The United States and the Taliban before and after 9/11

Jonathan Cristol

The United States and the Taliban before and after 9/11

palgrave
macmillan

Jonathan Cristol
Levermore Global Scholars Program
Adelphi University
Garden City, NY, USA

ISBN 978-3-319-97171-1   ISBN 978-3-319-97172-8   (eBook)
https://doi.org/10.1007/978-3-319-97172-8

Library of Congress Control Number: 2018951574

This Palgrave Pivot imprint is published by the registered company Springer Nature Switzerland AG
The registered company address is: Gewerbestrasse 11, 6330 Cham, Switzerland

If writing a book is a lonely process, then it is perhaps loneliest for its bystanders. Amanda Toronto, Lucy Cristol, and Milo Cristol bore the brunt of my physical and mental absence and they have been tolerant and forgiving.
This book is dedicated to them.

PREFACE

My first day of college was 3 August 1996. Some colleges may have had high speed internet then, but Bard College in rural Annandale-on-Hudson, New York, did not. There were two people in a room with one phone line. Such a thing is hard to imagine now. The internet was too slow to support graphics on the web, so we used a text-based browser called Lynx. Such a thing is even harder to imagine now. There was no information superhighway. It was an information creek. My main exposure to news of the outside world came each night at midnight when I listened to the BBC World Service on the local National Public Radio station. That was the first time I heard of the Taliban. For those first few weeks of college, I listened as the Taliban got closer and closer to Kabul, Afghanistan's capital, and I remember when Kabul fell on 27 September 2001. And at some point, soon after, I found other things to do in college besides lie in bed listening to the BBC.

In my second semester of graduate school at Yale University, I attended a debate between Sayed Rahmatullah Hashemi, an advisor to Taliban leader Mullah Mohammed Omar, and Harold Koh, a professor at Yale Law School who later became assistant secretary of state for human rights in the Obama Administration. Professor Koh spoke in legal and academic terms. His arguments were based in theory and legality. Mr. Rahmatullah articulated his positions clearly and convincingly. His arguments were rooted in the reality on the ground. Koh was clearly correct on the merits, but Rahmatullah handily won the debate. There was a reception for the foreign dignitary upstairs where I discovered that the

Taliban were regular people, and not the monsters I'd believed them to be. Rahmatullah was neither a naive simpleton nor a cartoon dictator. It was my first taste of public diplomacy and lessons from the experience stick with me more than 17 years later.

On my way to Prof. Jon Butler's class, "Religion and Modernity in Europe and America," I heard a radio report that a plane had crashed into the World Trade Center. A terrible accident, we held class as normal and only afterward discovered what happened. The Taliban did not carry out 9/11, but they were back in the news. They refused to turn over Osama bin Laden, the mastermind of the attacks, and the United States invaded Afghanistan on 7 October 2001. Kabul fell (again) on 13 November 2001.

In the following years, I finished my M.A., got married, had a daughter, finished my Ph.D., and had a son. Now my children are in elementary school, the United States has 15,000 troops in Afghanistan, and the Taliban just agreed to a "ceasefire" for Eid al-Fitr, the holiday marking the end of the holy month of Ramadan. The quotation marks are because the Taliban said that the ceasefire did not apply to foreign forces.

After the US invasion of Afghanistan, I heard little about Washington's relationship with the Taliban before 9/11, but I knew one existed. I knew Rahmatullah did not travel from Kandahar just to talk to a bunch of Yale students. I wanted to learn more about that relationship, specifically why the US did not recognize the Taliban government as the legitimate government of Afghanistan when it could make a compelling legal case for recognition. President Bill Clinton's non-recognition of the Taliban government became a case study in my doctoral dissertation completed at the University of Bristol in 2012—"American Diplomatic Recognition and Classical Realist International Relations Theory." This book is an expansion of that case study.

I am a professional critic. I can explain why policymakers' decisions are bad without having to offer any helpful alternatives. In my dissertation, I argued that the Clinton Administration's non-recognition of the Taliban government was a mistake, and that it would have been better to recognize the Taliban government. My 2012 argument was that the Clinton Administration was too influenced by domestic politics, and that the influence of the Feminist Majority Foundation, while well meaning, was ultimately negative. The reality is more complicated.

The US and the Taliban held countless meetings, in Afghanistan, in Pakistan, and even in the United States, but could never come to a workable arrangement. The Taliban's primary interest was for the US to extend diplomatic recognition to the Taliban government in Kabul. America's primary interest was for the Taliban to expel Osama bin Laden. This book examines both why diplomatic recognition was so important to the Taliban government and why the US refused to recognize it. It is a story about people making reasonable and defensible decisions that ultimately led to poor policy outcomes.

Chapter 1 focuses on diplomatic recognition of new governments, the competing theories of diplomatic recognition, and the benefits that come from recognition. Chapter 2 is about the rise of the Taliban and the possibility of a positive and productive relationship between the Taliban and the US. Chapter 3 is a history of US/Taliban relations from the fall of Kabul until the Al Qaeda attacks on the US embassies in Kenya and Tanzania. Chapter 4 examines how the US/Taliban relationship evolved in the first year after the embassy attacks. It shows that while the Clinton Administration outwardly opposed recognizing the Taliban government due to its treatment of women, behind-the-scenes it was willing to prioritize bin Laden at the expense of women's rights. Chapter 5 focuses on the deterioration in relations in the two years prior to 9/11. Chapter 6 focuses on 9/11 and the US invasion of Afghanistan. I argue that there was a very brief window in which US recognition of the Taliban government might have prevented Al Qaeda from taking root in Afghanistan, but by 1997 the opportunity had passed and Omar's obstinance meant there was no chance the US would ever recognize the Taliban government. I conclude that President George W. Bush erred by treating terrorists "and those who harbor them" the same way and that the 2001 invasion and occupation of Afghanistan could have been avoided.

The book is almost entirely based on publicly available primary sources and contemporaneous accounts including: declassified government documents, primarily from the State Department and Central Intelligence Agency and located at the National Security Archive at George Washington University; congressional hearing transcripts; presidential speeches and press conferences; and United Nations Security Council transcripts. Some of these had not yet been declassified when I wrote my dissertation. The documents tell a different story than I had anticipated.

This is a story about bad options.

New York City, USA   Jonathan Cristol
June 2018

ACKNOWLEDGEMENTS

I could not have written this book without the help of some great people and institutions.

The Levermore Global Scholars (LGS) program at Adelphi University provided financial and administrative support for the research and writing of this book. I am especially grateful to Peter DeBartolo, Cindy Maguire, and Michelle Schneider for making LGS such a welcoming environment. The World Policy Institute (WPI) has been my home for the past three years, and I am particularly grateful to Kate Maloff for her outstanding leadership and support for my work. Rachel Meyer, Jonathan Becker, Jim Ketterer, and Julia Tinneny at Bard College gave me (literal) space to finish writing and editing the book. Jutta Weldes is a tough reader, harsh critic, and good friend. Her guidance over many years improved my writing, my research, and my analytical thinking. Andy Reiter helped me navigate the peer review process. Vanessa Bobadilla provided the technical means to finish writing. Stephanie Carvin explained how to read Canadian government document headers. Giles Alston was literally relentless in encouraging me to write a book. Joel Rosenthal has been a great friend and mentor for over 15 years. My CNN and *World Policy Journal* editors Yaffa Fredrick, Kirsi Goldynia, Laurel Jarombek, and Luke McGee all made me a better writer. Yunju Ko, Kim Lalley, David Pavey, and Cynthia Wong's confidence in me is deeply meaningful, and hopefully not misplaced. Bridget Coggins' work is always ten steps ahead of my own and she is an intellectual trailblazer. Obviously Gruber. The late James Chace inspired my love of diplomatic history and international relations theory. Jeremy Cristol is the kind of doctor who can actually help people, and his help with my wrist made it physically possible to write this book. He is also an incredibly generous and loving brother. Rebecca Kittell and James Cristol provided just the right amount of parental encouragement without crossing the line into micromanagement. Hopefully, I will be able to find that line with my own children.

I have been extraordinarily fortunate to benefit from several outstanding research assistants. Madeline de Figueiredo, Anusha Prasad, and Alana Sheppard provided valuable assistance for the original book proposal. Sona Lim, Kayla Straub, Zuwaina Ateig, and Ji Won Lim helped with all of my assorted, simultaneous projects. I am especially grateful to Nada Osman, my LGS research assistant, and Mashell Rahimzadeh, my WPI research assistant. Ms. Osman spent months tracking down sources and collating and organizing thousands of pages of government documents, congressional testimony, UN transcripts, and academic articles. She is reliable and diligent and this could not have been done without her. Ms. Rahimzadeh fact-checked dates, names, and places, and found answers to dozens and dozens of my questions. She is a brilliant copyeditor, artful writer, and excellent guide to Afghan culture. The book is much better because of her help. I am looking forward to seeing great things from all of my past and present RAs (no pressure!). Most importantly, any typos, errors, or inaccuracies are mine and mine alone.

This book began as a chapter of my doctoral dissertation at the University of Bristol under the supervision of Jutta Weldes and Elke Krahmann. I am grateful to them and to my outside examiners Anthony Lang and Ryerson Christie for their valuable comments. Portions of this book were presented as papers at the American Political Science Association Annual Convention in 2010 and at the International Studies Association (ISA) Annual Conventions in 2008 and 2010. I am grateful to the people who showed up and asked tough questions at those panels. The anonymous reviewers for Palgrave gave thoughtful, thorough, and helpful comments.

It was at the ISA 2017 Convention in Baltimore that I met my editor, Anca Pusca, from Palgrave Macmillan. I am grateful to her and to Katelyn Zingg for their encouragement, time, energy, and putting up with my (hopefully relatively brief) delays and my (almost certainly annoying) questions!

Lucy Cristol and Milo Cristol have put up with their father's mental and physical absence for most of their lives. They managed it wonderfully and they are always (kinda) interested in what I am doing, though I suspect they would be happier if I was writing a *Who Was?* book or a My Little Pony graphic novel.

Nothing I do would be possible without the love and support (and editorial guidance) of the brilliant writer Amanda R. Toronto. When she's not around, I, to borrow her phrase, "literally go off the rails." I'm not sure how many wives would tolerate their husband saying, "I need to go away for a week on Tuesday but I can't tell you where and I won't know myself until I get there," or, more frequently, their husband sitting at the dinner table with his face in the computer. I appreciate it. You put up with a lot. I love you.

Thank you all.

CONTENTS

AUTHOR'S NOTE

Every book involves choices. Here are a few that I made and why I made them.

I cite most government documents without using page or paragraph numbers. If you have ever looked at a pdf of a State Department cable you will understand why. The pagination is confusing and there are multiple options from which to choose. None of the documents are so long that the lack of page or paragraph number presents a problem. **I use uniform, popular spellings across the text, quotes, citations, and titles**. For example, "Osama bin Laden" is popularly spelled with an "O," but in many government documents it is spelled with a "U." I have standardized the spelling without indication in each instance. And speaking of Osama bin Laden, I refer to him as "bin Laden," in deference to the popular nomenclature and not as "Osama," which would be more culturally appropriate. **I have standardized the spelling of Afghan names**. The names are transliterated and the spelling is often the choice of the author, so for readability, I have used the most common spelling for each person or name. **A note on Afghan naming**: The second component of male names is often treated as a last name. For example, I refer to Sayed Rahmatullah Hashemi as "Rahmatullah," and Wakil Ahmed Muttawakil as "Ahmed." **A note on State Department documents**: I have attributed authorship of State Department documents to the person who signed the document, but the reader should be aware that it is often the case that the document was actually written by someone of a lower rank.

CHAPTER 1

Introduction: Diplomatic Recognition and the Taliban Movement

Abstract Recognition was the top foreign policy priority of the new Taliban movement in Afghanistan. This chapter answers two questions: What is diplomatic recognition? and Why was American diplomatic recognition so important to the Taliban? The chapter explains the different theoretical and legal criteria that states use to recognize new regimes or new states. It investigates the tangible and intangible benefits that come from diplomatic recognition. Recognition legitimates the authority of the government for the domestic audience. Domestic legitimacy was especially important to the Taliban, who were engaged in a civil war for the majority of their tenure. It argues that the United States adheres to a constitutive theory of diplomatic recognition and recognizes new governments for political, rather than legal, reasons. It did not recognize the Taliban government for domestic political reasons and a misperception of the geostrategic importance of Afghanistan after the Cold War.

Keywords Afghanistan · Diplomatic recognition · Effective control Legitimacy · Taliban · United States foreign policy

In 1994, the Afghan government was an amalgam of different *mujahedeen* groups armed by the United States to fight the Soviet Union in the 1979–1989 Soviet–Afghan War. The *mujahedeen's* tenure in power was marked by constant armed conflict between factions, which resulted in little stability for the average Afghan. The instability was so

© The Author(s) 2019

J. Cristol, *The United States and the Taliban before and after 9/11*, https://doi.org/10.1007/978-3-319-97172-8_1

1

great that at one point, Prime Minister Gulbuddin Hekmatyar, the recognized prime minister of Afghanistan, "threatened to destroy his own capital city" (Gannon 2005, p. 12). Hekmatyar was a friend of Saudi terrorist Osama bin Laden and had a horrifying human rights record. One Defense Intelligence Agency raw-intelligence report called Hekmatyar an, "incompetent… Islamic fundamentalist who reportedly boasted about throwing acid in the faces of women who did not wear the traditional, all-covering, Afghan chador" (Anonymous. Redacted. 2001). Burhanuddin Rabbani, the recognized president of Afghanistan, believed that Afghanistan should be governed according to Islamic law. A United States Senate Resolution singled out his forces for "numerous abhorrent human rights abuses, including the rape, sexual abuse, torture, abduction, and persecution of women and girls" (Dodd 1997, par. 3).[1] This was the government recognized by the United States as the legitimate government of Afghanistan at the start of the Taliban movement.

This chapter looks at two questions: What is diplomatic recognition? and Why did the Taliban care so much about the United States recognizing the Taliban government? Though the Taliban did not formally request recognition until 8 November 1996, it was a top priority of its foreign policy from the founding of the movement until almost the day the US invasion of Afghanistan began on 7 October 2001. The Taliban did not seek recognition only from the United States. They also prioritized gaining control of Afghanistan's seat in the United Nations and sought recognition from a wide range of other governments as well. They were successful only in persuading Pakistan, Saudi Arabia, and the United Arab Emirates to grant diplomatic recognition to the Taliban. The Taliban did not desire recognition to gratify their own egos. Recognized states enjoy a particular set of rights and privileges.

Recognition is not "merely cognition" (Briggs 1949, p. 120). Diplomatic recognition is the process by which one state recognizes a particular political entity as a state, with all of the rights, privileges, duties, and obligations of statehood. Diplomatic recognition is not only extended to new states, but also to new governments that come to power through irregular means (typically, but not always, violent). Recognition of a state is recognition of its *existence*. Recognition of a government is recognition of its *legitimacy*. In 1979, the Islamic Republic of Iran required re-recognition as Iran's legitimate government, but the sovereign state of Iran remained recognized. The Taliban capture of Kabul, and later 90% of Afghanistan's territory, presented the world with a similar situation—Afghanistan did not require re-recognition, but so long as the Taliban were unrecognized, President Burhanuddin Rabbani's government remained recognized as the legitimate government of Afghanistan despite controlling only 10% of Afghanistan's territory.[2]

There are two sets of generally accepted criteria for what constitutes a state. The first criteria originate from the 1933 "Montevideo Convention on the Rights and Duties of States," which defined a state as an entity that has (1) a permanent population, (2) a defined territory, (3) a government, and (4) the capacity to enter into external relations with other states, meaning that it has an independent foreign policy. The second set of criteria comes from "Agenda Item 61" of the (1950) Fifth Session of the United Nations General Assembly. The UN criteria, more applicable to recognition of new governments than states and thus, more relevant to the Taliban question, define states as entities that have (1) "effective control and authority over all or nearly all the national territory," (2) "obedience of the bulk of the population," and (3) the "control, authority, and obedience appear to be of a permanent character." Neither of these sets of criteria have anything to do with democracy, or liberal government. The people do not even have to be supportive of the government; they could tacitly acquiesce to the government's authority. At its peak, the Taliban government exerted "effective control" over "nearly all the national territory," its presence appeared permanent, and the bulk of the population was not in rebellion against it. The fact that the Taliban government met these criteria did not automatically entitle it to recognition from the United States.

Afghanistan under the Taliban clearly met the Montevideo criteria for statehood, and Afghanistan's continued existence as a sovereign state was never in dispute. The Taliban's qualifications for recognition as the legitimate government of Afghanistan under the UN criteria are more arguable as the Taliban never succeeded in pacifying the entirety of the state. The Taliban had a tougher case to make for it to be seated in the UN. Membership in the UN requires governments to be "willing and able to carry out UN charter obligations" (Blanchfield and Browne 2014, p. 5). It is clear that the Taliban were not able to meet these obligations and they likely did not even understand what they were. Australian National University's William Maley (2000, par. 18) writes that the Taliban had, "Little understanding of the evolved practices of modern diplomacy; virtually no comprehension of the politics of states outside the Muslim world." The desire for recognition was intuitive, not the result of knowledge of international law.

However, for all intents and purposes, for the United States, the decision to recognize a new state or new government is not the result of an objective assessment of specific criteria; it is a political decision. The United States adheres to the "constitutive theory of recognition"—a state exists when other states say it exists. There are those who argue that the United States should follow an alternate model—the "declaratory theory of recognition." This theory sees recognition as a three-step process: (1) a political entity declares itself a new state or in control of a preexisting state; (2) the potential recognizer applies some set of preexisting criteria for statehood to the new entity; and (3) if it meets those criteria it is recognized; if it does not meet those criteria, it is not recognized. Thus, recognition is either automatic or unnecessary. Automatic because a government needs only to meet the criteria to be recognized, and unnecessary because if it meets objective criteria, there is no need to internationally validate a government with recognition. Thomas Jefferson was a supporter of the declarative approach to recognition, as he did not think the United States should make political judgments about foreign governments (Weeks 2001). Successive American presidents shared Jefferson's position until President Woodrow Wilson changed US policy for ideological reasons.

The most common *approach* to recognition in either theory is "effectivism"—the idea that a government that is "in actual control of the administrative machinery of the state, is performing normal governmental functions, and is not meeting with open resistance to its authority" is the legitimate government of the state (Fenwick 1944, p. 448). The lack of open resistance helps to indicate to the states in the system that the new government is legitimate. The French justified recognition of the United States as a response to the "effective possession of independence" after the American Revolution (Fabry 2010, p. 30). Nevertheless, Georgia Institute of Technology's Mikulas Fabry (2010, p. 41) argues that, "The ability to take effective control of a territory, whether from within or without, could not, by itself establish legitimate titles." Historically, effective control was a necessary, but not sole, condition for recognition. A state is not compelled by international law to recognize *any* government that has effective control, but legally it cannot recognize one that does not. There is, however, an "effectivist" *theory* of diplomatic recognition—that if a new government has effective control over its territory, then it *is* the state's legitimate government, regardless of its character. Thus, effectivism is similar to the declaratory theory, but is specific about the requirement for recognition to be granted.[3] Yet even effectivism is not widely practiced. If effectivism were widely practiced, then, at the apex of their power, the Taliban would have been recognized by more than three states.

The declaratory approach to recognition may seem simpler, but despite specific sets of criteria used by states, multiple states that do not meet those criteria have been universally recognized and indisputably exist. University of California at Santa Barbara's Bridget Coggins (2006, p. 10) writes, "There are very few cases in recent history where new state members unambiguously met the theoretical or legal standards for statehood, yet states have proliferated." And while the declaratory approach may *seem* simpler, between 1931 and 2002 only four states (Bangladesh, Eritrea, Slovenia, and Somaliland) met the criteria for statehood yet only three of those were recognized, along with a myriad of others (Coggins 2006, p. 89).

Fabry (2010, p. 14) argues that the current, political approach to recognition is arbitrary and that, "It is doubtful that there is any sustainable basis for recognizing states other than the one suggested by the nineteenth-century Anglo-American doctrine, namely de facto statehood." James Crawford (2006, p. 93), a judge at the International Court of Justice, agrees, writing that, "An entity is not a state because it is recognized; it is recognized because it is a state." Coggins (2006) reaches a different conclusion, arguing that political acts of recognition provide a sound basis for recognition decisions.

The constitutive theory of recognition is far more reflective of reality than its objectivist rival. Statehood and legitimacy are not connected to objective criteria. A political entity becomes a state when others say that it is a state. A government is legitimate when others say it is legitimate. Recognition constitutes statehood and/or legitimacy. In practice, states recognize new governments for specific reasons. Coggins (2006, pp. 19–20) offers four scenarios in which a state would have cause to offer recognition: (1) when there is geostrategic benefit; (2) when domestic politics makes recognition the preferred policy; (3) when international norms dictate that recognition *should* be offered; and (4) when there is some sort of kinship between peoples. Coggins' scenarios help explain why the US never recognized the Taliban government. There was a misperception of the geostrategic benefit to recognition of the Taliban government. American domestic politics made recognition exceedingly difficult. The Taliban violated a wide range of international norms, from the 1971 Vienna Convention on Diplomatic Relations to the 1979 International Convention Against the Taking of Hostages, and most famously their horrifying treatment of women and girls. And while the US had armed and aided the *mujahedeen* in their fight against the Soviet Union, there was little blood or battle kinship.

Decisions to recognize a new state or new government are made based on ideological grounds all the time. That states are recognized simply because they de facto exist is a fiction that is hard to maintain, and a close look at the map should serve to dispel such notions. Indeed, there are ten self-declared independent political entities that have been functioning independently for years including Somaliland, Taiwan, and Western Sahara (Geldenhuys 2009, p. 2). Recognition provides tangible and intangible benefits to a new government, which is why every new government desires recognition. Recognition provides "pivotal legitimacy" to a government's claim to sovereignty (Coggins 2006, p. 18). Perhaps the most important benefit that comes from recognition is "sovereignty." A sovereign, recognized government can refuse entry to foreign forces, can negotiate and enter into international agreements, and can join international organizations and call on them to act inside its territory. This could mean assisting in suppressing an insurgency or providing humanitarian assistance. In practice, this may not be so clear cut—the Taliban were themselves the insurgency in Afghanistan, until, arguably, they were not, but the United Nations and a variety of aid groups worked and reached agreements with the Taliban anyway. A recognized government is entitled to state assets in foreign banks. This was an issue for the Taliban, who wanted access to Afghan money held internationally. A recognized government enjoys the extraterritoriality of its embassies and consulates and its diplomats enjoy immunity, at least within those states that recognize it. Only a recognized government can borrow money from the World Bank or the International Monetary Fund (IMF), which can have the result of keeping unrecognized governments in a particularly precarious financial situation. Recognition also confers obligations on the recognized government. For example, it must abide by treaties and it is bound by international law (Crawford 2006).

These are not only some of the major tangible benefits for a recognized government in the international community, but there are also intangible internal and external benefits for a recognized government.

For relatively weak states, internal, intangible benefits may actually be the most important of all. The most important internal, intangible benefit is legitimacy. The people can consider governments legitimate if they meet their needs and provide basic services to the population. In order to meet these needs, states must acquire tangible resources. These resources can be extracted from either the people or from other states. But they can only extract resources from other states if those states recognize it. Legitimacy can also come from the government gaining power through free and fair elections, at least for adherents to the idea of "democratic legitimacy."

Recognition can enhance a government's chance for survival if it happens quickly and is widely reported (Peterson 1982, p. 329). Conversely, non-recognition can make life difficult for the government involved, particularly if it is militarily weak or lacks desirable natural resources. If a potential recognizer does not favor the new government, it can both withhold recognition and provide aid to the previous government. This is perfectly acceptable so long as the recognizer acknowledges that sovereignty is still contested and it has chosen to back the original government. However, the recognizer cannot continue to recognize the original government once it has lost "effective control" of its territory. University of Massachusetts at Amherst's M.J. Peterson (1982, p. 332) writes that such recognition is "clearly illegal because it willfully ignores the absence of effective control." This situation is called "prolonged recognition."[4] Despite the illegality of this diplomatic tactic, there are examples of it throughout American diplomatic history. The United States recognized the Chinese nationalists as sovereign over mainland China long after it lost effective control to the communists; and the US continued to recognize the government of Burhanuddin Rabbani in Afghanistan long after he had lost effective control to the Taliban.

Powerful countries can be expected to extract resources from other states to benefit their own constituents, while weaker states must rely on "external validation" to remain in power. As Dartmouth College's Michael Mastanduno et al. (1989, p. 464) writes, "For new states (i.e., those that have come to power in the wake of internal revolutions), external validation involves first and foremost diplomatic recognition. Gaining recognition of the international community appears to be an exceptionally powerful means for a nascent state to establish legitimacy in the eyes of the *domestic* population." Thus it is important for most non-Marxist revolutionary governments to show their people that it is no longer a revolutionary insurgency, uprising, or political group, but it has been accepted as the legitimate government of the state and thus the people should now treat it as such. This could be why, as Maley (2000, par. 15) writes, "The first broad policy objective of the Taliban was to win acceptance as a government." Recognition legitimates the authority of the government for the domestic audience. Domestic legitimacy was especially important to the Taliban who were engaged in a civil war against the "United Islamic Front for the Salvation of Afghanistan," more widely known as the "Northern Alliance," for the majority of their tenure.[5]

NOTES

1. Abdul Rashid Dostum, leader of the National Islamic Movement of Afghanistan, was cited alongside Rabbani.
2. Burhanuddin Rabbani was assassinated in his Kabul home on 20 September 2011 (Rubin 2011).
3. Switzerland and Britain have advocated formally changing the practice of recognition to an effectivist approach, but they also include democracy as a necessary factor for recognition (Grant 1998–1999, p. 444).
4. See M.J. Peterson (1997, Chapter 3) for further discussion of "prolonged recognition."
5. The Taliban also faced opposition from other groups throughout Afghanistan.

REFERENCES

Anonymous. Redacted. 2001. [Redacted]/Veteran Afghanistan Traveler's Analysis of Al Qaeda and Taliban Exploitable Weaknesses [from Defense Intelligence Agency to [redacted]]. 3 October 2001. Defense Intelligence Agency, document accessed at the National Security Archive, Washington, DC.

Blanchfield, Luisa, and Marjorie Ann Browne. 2014. Membership in the United Nations and Its Specialized Agencies. R43614, Congressional Research Service, 19 June 2014.

Briggs, Herbert W. 1949. Recognition of States: Some Reflections on Doctrine and Practice. The American Journal of International Law 43 (1): 113–121.

Coggins, Bridget. 2006. Secession, Recognition and the International Politics of Statehood. PhD dissertation, Columbus, OH, The Ohio State University.

Crawford, James. 2006. *The Creation of States in International Law*, 2nd ed. New York: Oxford University Press.

Dodd, Christopher. 1997. Senate Concurrent Resolution 6. 7 February 1997, 105th Congress, 1st Session. Government Publications Office.

Fabry, Mikulas. 2010. *Recognizing States: International Society & the Establishment of New States Since 1776*. New York: Oxford University Press.

Fenwick, C.G. 1944. The Recognition of New Governments Instituted by Force. *The American Journal of International Law* 38 (3): 448–452.

Gannon, Kathy. 2005. *I Is for Infidel*. New York: Public Affairs.

Grant, Thomas D. 1998. Defining Statehood: The Montevideo Convention and Its Discontents. *Columbia Journal of Transnational Law* 37: 403–457.

Geldenhuys, Deon. 2009. *Contested States in World Politics*. New York: Palgrave Macmillan.

Maley, William. 2000. The Foreign Policy of the Taliban. Report, Council on Foreign Relations. 15 February 2000. Web.

Mastanduno, Michael, et al. 1989. Toward a Realist Theory of State Action. *International Studies Quarterly* 33 (4): 457–474.

Peterson, M.J. 1982. Political Use of Recognition: The Influence of the International System. *World Politics* 34 (3): 324–352.

Peterson, M.J. 1997. *Recognition of Governments: Legal Doctrine and State Practice, 1815–1995*. Basingstoke, UK: Macmillan.

Rubin, Alissa J. 2011. Assassination Deals Blow to Peace Process in Afghanistan. *New York Times*, 20 September 2011. Web.

Weeks, Gregory. 2001. Almost Jeffersonian: US Recognition Policy Toward Latin America. *Presidential Studies Quarterly* 31 (3): 490–504.

CHAPTER 2

The Rise of the Taliban

Abstract The Taliban were founded by Mullah Mohammed Omar in the mid-1990s. The specifics of the origin story vary between sources, but one thing is certain—the Taliban rapidly expanded their territorial control. The United States needed to know who this new group was and began regular meetings with the Taliban in early 1995. This chapter explores the rise of the Taliban and the US relationship with the Taliban from the start of the movement until the fall of Kabul in September 1996. In this time period, the US and the Taliban had a cordial relationship; but the US was concerned both about women's rights under the Taliban and about the Taliban's obvious unwillingness to seek a negotiated settlement with Afghanistan's weak central government.

Keywords Afghanistan · Diplomacy · Mullah Mohammed Omar
Taliban · United States foreign policy

The Taliban were formed by Mullah Mohammed Omar.[1] Omar was a man of few words, with an "idiosyncratic almost obscurantist, style of leadership" (Simons 1997c). He focused on the big picture, and let others handle the implementation of his policies. One visitor described him as "Uninspiring, without charisma. He had no idea what was going on in the world. He knew only jihad" (Filkins 2001, par. 36). His exact age was never known with certainty. CIA documents say he was born in 1960, but United Nations documents list his birth as 1950 ("Security

© The Author(s) 2019   11
J. Cristol, *The United States and the Taliban before and after 9/11*,
https://doi.org/10.1007/978-3-319-97172-8_2

Council Committee Concerning" 2001). A confidential source told US Political Officer Eric Kunsman (1996) that Omar was from, "The Khotak tribe, which is not very important. This insulates him from the tribal rivalry within [the] Taliban." Omar was humble and he was respected.

Omar began the group from a mosque in Sanjli in southern Afghanistan. He, like the other Taliban leadership, was a rural man, not used to places like Kabul, or even to small towns in the more liberal north. In the north, educated women walked around uncovered. They worked in the professions. Schulz and Schulz (1999, p. 243) write that before the Taliban takeover, 60% of Kabul University teachers, 70% of school teachers, 50% of civilian government workers, and 40% of doctors were women. Kabul even had an active nightlife. This milieu would have been completely alien to Omar.

Life was harder in the rural, lawless south. Omar was fed up with the lawlessness and crime and decided to take matters into his own hands. That much is clear. The specifics of his rise vary between accounts. Perhaps the most common origin story of Mullah Omar and the Taliban is that, whenever Omar left Sanjli, he encountered roadblocks run by bandits demanding money. Fed up with banditry and extortion, he gathered together other mullahs and marched on a checkpoint. Their success in dismantling the checkpoint attracted followers and further success, which begat further success, and led to the creation of an armed movement against what Omar saw as Kabul's corruption. The original group was made up of 60 mullahs, but their students soon joined them and thus the group became known as "the students," or "Taliban" (Gannon 2005, p. 31). At least, that is one widely accepted possible origin story.

Another account was given by a Taliban official to US Ambassador to Pakistan John Cameron Monjo. He told him that the Taliban began, "At the *madrasa* of a prominent trader [and Omar's former commander], Haji Bashar" (Monjo 1995b).[2] Mullah Omar was not the most distinguished scholar, nor was he "particularly charismatic nor articulate," but he "earned a reputation for bravery... honesty, and sincerity." After some fellow students were gang-raped by a commander and his men, Omar had a vision of the Prophet Mohammed, who told him to bring peace to Afghanistan. Bashar raised $250,000 for Omar and contributed six pick-up trucks (Monjo 1995b). The *New York Times'* Dexter Filkins (2001, par. 33) corroborated part of that story reporting that Omar's original offensive was against "a group of warlords who had raped and shaved the head of a girl." Later Filkins (2008, p. 30) wrote that Omar "decided he'd had enough" when he witnessed "two warlords fighting over the rights to a very young boy."

Another common and compelling argument is that the Taliban were the creation of Pakistan's Inter Services Intelligence Directorate (ISI) and were armed, trained, and funded directly by Pakistan. In this version of events, the original 60 mullahs came from madrassas in Pakistan and exploited the ethnic kinship of Pakistani and Afghan Pashtuns to create a new force in southern Afghanistan. Barnett Rubin (1998, par. 20), arguably the world's leading expert on Afghanistan, said that the Taliban, "Succeeded largely because of the military aid they received from Pakistan."

The Taliban were not unpopular. One report stated that when the Taliban first achieved victories they were "warmly welcomed," but have "closed down girls' schools, sent working women home and set up strict Islamic courts. Spokesmen have declared television, drugs and elections un-Islamic." The same report says that the leadership is unclear beyond Omar, and the composition of the approximately eight man ruling body "changes frequently" (MacFarquhar 1995, pars. 7–9). There was much that was unknown about the group, its leader, and its leadership.

The United States did not know enough about the Taliban and needed to find out more. Because the US embassy in Kabul had been closed since 1989, the job was primarily tasked to the US embassy in Islamabad and the US consulate in Peshawar. On 3 November 1994, US Consul General in Peshawar Richard Henry Smyth sent Secretary of State Warren Christopher a cable about this new group. Smyth, aided by still-classified sources, provides one of the earliest histories of the Taliban. His account differs from those discussed above: Mullah Omar's "Taliban" was actually the second group operating under that name in Kandahar. The first was led by Mullah Yar Mohammad. The second, then known as the "New Taliban," was founded by Mullah Omar and his deputy Mullah Ehsanullah Ehsan.[3] The new group's initial goal was quite modest—to "'clean up' the Chaman-Kandahar Highway" and its first victory was over a freelance commander named Fatah Mohammad who extorted drivers along the road. He was defeated, tried, and hung. After that incident, "Independent toll stations along [that] highway reportedly drastically reduced in number," and the Taliban continued to clear the roads. According to Smyth, Ehsanullah told the BBC that their goals were to "open the highway to free traffic" and remove the

"Wahhabi and Salafi influence" from the area. Smyth could not be certain if they did or did not receive support from Pakistan—"The Taliban have been characterized as being simultaneously Pakistani tools and anti-Pakistan"—but concluded by saying, "If the Taliban was created by secular or outside forces, however, it is very possible that their backers may find that they have created a tiger that is more than willing to take independent action and not be anyone's tool." One of Smyth's most interesting observations was that the Taliban were, "largely drawn from religious students who *did not fight in the jihad* [emphasis added]" (Smyth 1994).

Just a few weeks later, on 28 November 1994, Monjo sent another long cable to Secretary Christopher about the new player in Kandahar. He was still not certain about the extent of Pakistan's involvement in the creation of the Taliban—"The origins, goals and sponsors of the 'Taliban'... movement remain unclear, even to well-informed Afghans"—but reached a different conclusion about their military background. Monjo wrote that the Taliban was a group that, "Fought with distinction against the Soviets" and were then "re-mobilized through a combination of frustration with extortionist party commanders and foreign financing—probably by conservative religious groups in Pakistan." These discrepancies show just how little was known about the Taliban at the time.

Different declassified documents from 1994 focus primarily on the role of Pakistan in the Taliban's creation and its military success and reach different conclusions. One thing that all early accounts agree on was that, regardless of the origin story, Pakistan would be unlikely to effectively control the Taliban. State Department Bureau of South Asian Affairs official R.L. Chew (circa. 1996) wrote in a document on Pakistan/Afghanistan relations that while, "Pakistan has given material and tactical support to the Taliban.... Privately they admit they do not want to see the Taliban in power in Kabul." Pakistan may have wanted the Taliban to be included in the government, but did not want them to *be* the government. It was not until 1998 that Pakistan admitted that it had been arming the Taliban, though when it started to do so remains unclear (Simons 1998a).

Information about the Taliban was much easier to come by in 1995. They had gained in strength and popularity. Mullah Omar began giving interviews to the BBC. John Holzman (1995a), the US Deputy Chief of Mission in Islamabad reported back to Washington that the Taliban were "Well-armed, militarily proficient, and eager to expand their influence." Holzman heard from multiple sources that the Taliban intended to continue on to Kabul and "as much of the rest of Afghanistan as possible." The Taliban claimed to have 4000 paid fighters, 100 operational tanks, 11 MIG fighters, and nine transport helicopters. The source of funding was still a major question for the United States. "The apparent gap between obvious sources of funding and expenditures suggests to our interlocutors that the Taliban have other benefactors," wrote Holzman (1995a). The Taliban were observed to be orderly and disciplined, at least, relative to the other Afghan factions. Two other features of the Taliban had become clear to the Americans. They practiced and intended to enforce a stark brand of Islam—in Kandahar they banned chess, marbles, and the presence of women outside of the home—and they were concerned about and opposed to "Iranian influence" (Holzman 1995a).

The United States was eager to speak to the Taliban and, using the United Nations as an intermediary (there was not yet a Taliban representative in Peshawar), arranged what was perhaps the first direct meeting between American officials and the Taliban. The meeting was held on 13 February 1995. The political officers from the US embassy in Islamabad and the US consulate in Peshawar traveled to Kandahar and met with seven Taliban officials including Kandahar mayor Maulavi Abul-Abbas and UN Affairs and Foreign Visitors chief Mullah Attiqullah.

The meeting began with a prayer for the "conversion of the unbelievers." Abul-Abbas informed the Americans that the Taliban's goals were the disarmament of all the commanders, establishment of sharia, and a single government in Afghanistan. This meeting clearly established that the Taliban aimed to take over the country. Abul-Abbas said that, "Anyone who gets in our way will be crushed" (Monjo 1995a).

The Taliban representatives were much less forthcoming with information than in subsequent meetings, though that could be because they did not have answers to the Americans' questions. One focus of US/Taliban relations was established in this very first meeting—the issue of opium poppy crops in the country that was the world's leading supplier of opium. The US offered the Taliban participation in a counter-narcotics training program, but the Taliban declined. "The Taliban shura will not let the people grow drugs," said Abul-Abbas (Monjo 1995a). This statement was met with some opposition by other Taliban present and the mayor walked it back and pointed out that it was an economic issue and economic alternatives were needed before more could be done to stop poppy growth. The mayor did agree to further discussion with the US on this issue. The comment at the end of the memorandum of the conversation says, "The overall impression was one of disingenuity and a degree of deception" (Monjo 1995a).

The two sides met again just days later in Peshawar. A still-classified source contacted the embassy in Islamabad and said that a still-classified senior Taliban official was in town for introductory meetings with the UN and other "friendly elements." The official met with the consulate's political officer on 17 February 1995. He asked that the meeting remain confidential as the Taliban were wary of being perceived to be influenced by outsiders, but the US was, "An important and unbiased friend." The participants in the meeting remain classified (Monjo 1995b).

The Taliban official described the structure of the Taliban and mentioned that the three most important people were Mullah Omar, Haji Bashar, and Kandahar governor Mohammed Hassan. There was a "high shura" of eight, and a 22 member shura. He said that the Taliban's goal was to disarm and unify Afghanistan. There could be elections in the future, but the Taliban shura would decide who could run in the elections. The US asked about drug eradication and he said that, in his home district, the Taliban had told the opium growers that they could no longer grow opium. On the subject of the United States, he said that, "The Taliban want very good relations with the US, particularly since the US had been so helpful in the jihad... The Taliban realize that the US and UN do not want to do anything but help the Afghans." The US official noticed that the Talib was "clearly well disposed towards the United States" (Monjo 1995b). This was a nice change in tone from the previous meeting and seemed to establish that the Taliban were not hostile to the United States. Assistant Secretary of State for South Asia Robin Raphel (1995, par. 9) testified to the Senate Foreign Relations Subcommittee on Near Eastern and South Asian Affairs that the Taliban's intentions were "unclear," but "its leadership has expressed support in principle for a peaceful political process."

The Taliban continued to expand their control of Afghanistan. On 3 September 1995, they took control of Shinand Air Base in Farah Province, and by the next day, the Taliban had taken the city of Herat. While months earlier, the Taliban claimed to have 4000 troops in total, according to an American citizen in Herat, there were now 3000–4000 troops in Herat alone. The Taliban take-over was described as "extremely well-disciplined and organized." The Taliban forces paid for anything they took from the market, and doubled the salary of the public serv-ants in Herat. The Taliban behaved in a "modest and dignified fashion." Omar addressed the city and was again described as "clearly uneducated" and without charisma. The Taliban were welcomed due to the prospects for stability and the belief that the US and UN backed them (Holzman 1995b). In fact, prominent anti-Taliban Afghans, like future foreign minister Abdullah Abdullah, believed that the United States was prop-ping up the Taliban (Gannon 2005, p. 3). That belief was not unique to Afghans, Moscow and Tehran both assumed that the US supported the Taliban (Christopher 1996). Local Tajiks also believed that the US was arming the Taliban, and saw early visits between US and Taliban offi-cials as corroborating evidence of that support. Kazakh diplomats were alleged to "believe the United States will recognize the Taliban regime because Washington seeks a pro-US regime in Kabul and less Russian and Iranian influence in Afghanistan" (Deutch 1996). The Kazakhs believed that other countries would follow America's lead in recognizing the Taliban.

Even the popular press acknowledged the importance of stability. John Lloyd (1996, p. 22) wrote in the *New Statesman*, "Afghanistan's Taliban regime is cruel and unsavory, but it could help end two dec-ades of murderous chaos. It is hard to see a group as ruthless and as repressive as the Taliban regime, which has taken power in Afghanistan, as a source of stability. But it may be one." In response to the chorus of voices claiming that Taliban stability was preferable to the chaos of the past, Lara Paul, writing in *Peace Magazine* (1997, p. 14), dissented, writing, "I doubt that Afghan women were asked for their opinion. For them, there is no peace." It had become clear that the Taliban's treat-ment of women was horrifying and unacceptable. However, the Taliban had diverging views on the treatment of women. Herat governor Yar Mohammed said that he would reopen schools for girls, but he was over-ruled by Kandahar (Kunsman 1996).

As the Taliban's military gains continued, the US hoped to bring them onboard with the UN political process. Many of the Taliban lead-ership were favorable to the UN plan for a coalition government, but Omar was opposed to a coalition and to the UN plan. Omar also had bigger concerns than the United States. He was concerned about a potential conflict with Iran and the Taliban placed "rocket launchers and artillery" on the Iranian border. The Taliban captured Iranian infiltrators and "told the Iranians that we are fully prepared to go inside Iran and fight" (Kunsman 1996). Tension with Iran was one constant in an inconsistent and rapidly changing Taliban leadership.

As their advance continued, it became clear that the Taliban was concerned about how they were perceived in the United States. In April 1996, Raphel met with six Taliban leaders including Chief of Information and Culture Maulavi Amir Khan Mottaqi, who asked Raphel "to help improve their image in the international community" and asked that she "tell President Clinton and the West that we are not bad people." This was noted as a "concern about their image" that was "previously absent." The Taliban also "denied being human rights violators" (Simons 1996). Raphel did believe that the US should engage with the Taliban and told other UN member states that, "It is not in the interests of Afghanistan or any of us here that the Taliban be isolated" (Farrow 2018, p. 29). At that time, the US had no intention of isolating the Taliban and made every effort to reach out and discuss a wide range of issues.

The United States government was both readily aware that the Taliban could take over the embittered country and tacitly supportive of its so doing. President Rabbani had been unable to marshal popular support or to exert domestic sovereignty. In fact, a cable from the US Embassy in Islamabad to Secretary Christopher referred to the legitimacy of the Rabbani government as "highly questionable" (Simons 1996). The United States Government was still hoping that the civil war could be stopped and that a negotiated settlement could be reached between the Rabbani government, the Taliban, and the other armed factions that would later coalesce into the Northern Alliance, though it recognized the difficult task at hand (Simons 1996).

Raphel returned to Washington to testify before the Senate Foreign Relations Committee's Subcommittee on Near Eastern and South Asian Affairs. She discussed the three major interests of the United States in Afghanistan. First, she cited regional stability, "We seek a negotiated peace in Afghanistan that would end its role as a battleground" (Raphel 1996, pp. 326–327). Second, she cited terrorism and narcotics, though narcotics formed the bulk of her statement on the issues. Third were humanitarian issues; but, "The common thread of all of our interests in Afghanistan is the need to restore stability" (Raphel 1996, pp. 326–327). Because the Taliban were seen as a potential source of stability, the US was open to exploring the relationship and determining if peace could finally be achieved in Afghanistan.

In 1996, the United States needed a policy to govern its interaction with the Taliban. The goal was a "broad-based government" and the policy was, effectively, neutrality. "We will work with whatever government may eventually emerge in Kabul, holding it strictly accountable to international norms of conduct," wrote R.L. Chew (circa. 1996). The United States Senate expressed its own view of events in Afghanistan on 28 June 1996. Colorado Senator Hank Brown submitted a resolution that stated that the resolution of the conflict in Afghanistan should be a "top priority" for the United States. This policy was just as Raphel and Afghanistan Country Officer Ronald McMullen articulated in the *Harvard International Review* (1995, pars. 13–15), "US policy in Afghanistan has focused on promoting a peaceful political process and favors no Afghan faction, party, movement, or individual.... [the] United States will work with whatever government emerges in Kabul, holding it strictly accountable to international norms of conduct." The lack of a functioning government allowed for a profusion of terrorist training camps, which the US knew existed in Afghanistan as early as 1995, and a major increase in opium production. The proliferation of terrorism and narcotics is something that could not be addressed without stability in Afghanistan.

The United States had another interest in the stability of Afghanistan. Many sources argue that US tacit support for the Taliban was due to the American oil company Unocal's interest in building a pipeline through Afghanistan. Unocal had a plan to construct a 1040 mile long, 42″ diameter pipeline from Chardzhou, Turkmenistan through Afghanistan to the Pakistani coast capable of carrying 1 million barrels per day (Maresca 1998). The documentary evidence does not bear out that the pipeline was the prevailing reason for early tacit support for the Taliban.[4] Moreover, it was more important to the Taliban than it was to the United States. There are very few references to the pipeline in official sources, and those references are to the positive and negative political ramifications of a pipeline.

In a meeting in Moscow with Russian Deputy Foreign Minister Albert Chernyshev, Raphel said, "The United States Government now hopes that peace in the region will facilitate US business interests like the proposed Unocal gas pipeline" (Pickering 1996). This would have the effect of bypassing Iran and potentially harming their oil production and economy, something Iran was keenly aware of. On 7 July 1997, a still-classified source said to the US embassy in Islamabad that, "A specific source of anger for Iran... is their belief that the US is strongly backing the Taliban as a way to ensure that Unocal is able to build the oil and gas pipelines connecting central and south Asia through Afghanistan" (Simons 1997b). In a later document, a still-classified source says that Unocal had to consider the political and regional repercussions of any of its decisions in light of the "politically-charged" environment between Iran and Pakistan: "Every business decision Unocal or any other company considers in this region has to be carefully reviewed for its potential international repercussions" (Simons 1997a). And so, in that sense, Washington could not help but be involved; but there is no evidence to suggest that the US government put Unocal's interests over the American, or even Afghan, national interest.

The Taliban advance continued and, in the Taliban's success, Mullah Omar saw the hand of God. In an extremely rare public appearance, on 4 April 1996, Mullah Omar visited the Shrine of the Cloak inside the Friday Mosque in Kandahar. The shrine housed a cloak said to have been worn by the Prophet Mohammed. Omar put on the cloak and made the controversial decision to declare himself "King of the Faithful," the highest title in Islam (Anderson 2002, par. 14). His decision was supported by an election held by 1200 ulema in Kandahar between 20 March and 4 April 1996 (Rubin 1998, pars. 28–29).

Omar's declaration alienated many Muslim states just when the Taliban were poised to make a major victory (Gannon 2005, pp. 42–43). On 27 September 1996, the Taliban took Kabul and toppled the Burhanuddin Rabbani government. The Taliban established a government in Kabul with Mullah Mohammed Rabbani (no relation) as its head of government. Mullah Omar would be head of state and remain in Kandahar. Now that the Taliban controlled Afghanistan's capital, the majority of its territory, and the bulk of the population, it could set out on the task of convincing other states that the Taliban should be recognized as the legitimate government of Afghanistan. There was only one problem: Osama bin Laden had moved to Afghanistan.

Notes

1. "Mullah" is an amorphous term that indicates the person is a learned religious person or cleric, but there are no set qualifications or requirements to earn the title. It is a title of respect and not necessarily of achievement. "Maulavi" typically connotes someone with a formal religious qualification.

2. "Madrasa" literally means "school," but in the Afghanistan/Pakistan region the term is typically used to describe an elementary or secondary school that provides only religious education. Haji Bashar's *madrasa* belonged to the pan-Islamic, India-based, Deobandi school of Sunni Islam, which "exalted extreme austerity and the subjugation of women" (Filkins 2001, par. 47).

3. Ehsanullah Ehsan was killed in Mazar-i-Sharif in 1997 (Rashid 2010, p. 100).

4. The pipeline issue is a major focus of Rashid (2010). It is interesting to note that Ambassador Thomas Simons (1998b) referred to Rashid in a cable as "somewhat conspiratorial-minded."

References

Anderson, Jon L. 2002. After the Revolution: The City of Kandahar, Post-Taliban, is Full of Reminders That the Taliban Were Not What They Seemed to Be. *The New Yorker*, 28 January 2002, 77(45). Web.

Brown, Hank. 1996. Senate Resolution 275. 28 June 1996. 104th Congress, 2nd Session, United States Senate.

Chew R. L. circa. 1996. Pakistan–Afghanistan Relations. US Department of State, document accessed at the National Security Archive, Washington, DC.

Christopher, Warren. 1996. Pak Foreign Minister Asks US Cooperation on Afghanistan [Secretary of State Christopher to US Embassy Islamabad]. 21 February 1996. US Department of State, document accessed at the National Security Archive, Washington, DC.

Deutch, John M. 1996. Central Asian Reaction to Taliban's Takeover of Kabul. 9 October 1996. Central Intelligence Agency document accessed at the National Security Archive, Washington, DC.

Farrow, Ronan. 2018. *War on Peace: The End of Diplomacy and the Decline of American Influence*. New York: W. W. Norton.

Filkins, Dexter. 2001. The Legacy of the Taliban Is a Sad and Broken Land. *New York Times*, 31 December 2001. Web.

Filkins, Dexter. 2008. *The Forever War*. New York: Alfred A. Knopf.

Gannon, Kathy. 2005. *I Is for Infidel*. New York: Public Affairs.

Holzman, John. 1995a. The Taliban: What We've Heard [from US Embassy Islamabad to Secretary of State Christopher]. 26 January 1995. US Department of State, document accessed at the National Security Archive, Washington, DC.

Holzman, John. 1995b. Eyewitness to the Fall of Herat Says Taliban are Winning Hearts and Minds—For Now [from US Embassy Islamabad to Secretary of State Christopher]. 18 September 1995. US Department of State, document accessed at the National Security Archive, Washington, DC.

Kunsman, Eric. 1996. Afghanistan: Taliban Official Says Divisions Within Movement Growing; Predicts 'Fight with Iran' [from US Embassy Islamabad to Secretary of State Christopher]. 19 February 1996. US Department of State, document accessed at the National Security Archive, Washington, DC.

Lloyd, John. 1996. John Lloyd. *New Statesman*, 11 October 1996, 9(424), 22.

MacFarquhar, Emily. 1995. The Rise of the Taliban. *U.S. News & World Report*, 6 March 1995, 119(9), 64–65.

Maresca, John J. 1998. Testimony to the US Congress House of Representatives, Committee on International Relations, Subcommittee on Asia and the Pacific. 12 February 1998. 105th Congress Washington, DC.

Monjo, John Cameron. 1994. The Taliban—Who Knows What the Movement Means? [from US Embassy Islamabad to Secretary of State Christopher]. 28 November 1994. US Department of State, document accessed at the National Security Archive, Washington, DC.

Monjo, John Cameron. 1995a. Meeting with the Taliban in Kandahar: More Questions than Answers [from US Embassy Islamabad to Secretary of State Christopher]. 15 February 1995. US Department of State, document accessed at the National Security Archive, Washington, DC.

Monjo, John Cameron. 1995b. Finally, A Talkative Talib: Origins and Membership of the Religious Students' Movement [from US Embassy Islamabad to Secretary of State Christopher]. 20 February 1995. US Department of State, document accessed at the National Security Archive, Washington, DC.

Paul, Lara. 1997. Women in Danger in Afghanistan. *Peace Magazine*, September/October 1997, 13(5), 14.

Pickering, Thomas R. 1996. A/S Raphel Consultations with Deputy FM Chernyshev [from US Embassy Moscow to Secretary of State Christopher]. 13 May 1996. US Department of State, document accessed at the National Security Archive, Washington, DC.

Raphel, Robin. 1995. Statement by Robin Raphel, Assistant Secretary of State for South Asian Affairs, before the Senate Foreign Relations Subcommittee on Near Eastern and South Asian Affairs. 7 March 1995. Document accessed at Mount Holyoke College website.

Raphel, Robin. 1996. U.S. Interests in and Policy Toward Afghanistan: [6 June 1996] Statement before the Subcommittee on Near Eastern and South Asian Affairs of the Senate Foreign Relations Committee. *U.S. Department of State Dispatch*, 17 June 1996, 7(25), 326–327.

Raphel, Robin, and Ronald McMullen. 1995. Mired in Conflict. *Harvard International Review* 18 (1): 40–43.

Rashid, Ahmed. 2010. *Taliban: Militant Islam, Oil and Fundamentalism in Central Asia*, 2nd ed. New Haven: Yale University Press.

Rubin, Barnett. 1998. Testimony on the Situation in Afghanistan before the United States Senate Committee on Foreign Relations. *Council on Foreign Relations*, 8 October 1998. Web.

Schulz, John J., and Linda Schulz. 1999. The Darkest of Ages: Afghan Women Under the Taliban. *Peace and Conflict: Journal of Peace Psychology* 5 (3): 237–254.

Security Council Committee Concerning Afghanistan Designates Funds, Financial Resources of Taliban. 2001. *United Nations Press Release*, 13 April 2001, SC/6844.

Simons, Thomas W. 1996. A/S Raphel Discusses Afghanistan [from US Embassy Islamabad to Secretary of State Christopher]. 22 April 1996. US Department of State, document accessed at the National Security Archive, Washington, DC.

Simons, Thomas W. 1997a. Afghanistan and Sectarian Violence Contribute to a Souring of Pakistan's Relations with Iran [from US Embassy Islamabad to Secretary of State Albright]. 13 March 1997. US Department of State, document accessed at the National Security Archive, Washington, DC.

Simons, Thomas W. 1997b. Afghanistan: Observers Report Uptick in Support for Anti-Taliban Factions by Iran [from US Embassy Islamabad to Secretary of State Albright]. 7 July 1997. US Department of State, document accessed at the National Security Archive, Washington, DC.

Simons, Thomas W. 1997c. Afghanistan: Taliban Decision-Making and Leadership Structure [from US Embassy Islamabad to Secretary of State Albright]. 30 December 1997. US Department of State, document accessed at the National Security Archive, Washington, DC.

Simons, Thomas W. 1998a. Afghanistan: [Redacted] Describes Pakistan's Current Thinking [from US Embassy Islamabad to Secretary of State Albright]. 9 March 1998. US Department of State, document accessed at the National Security Archive, Washington, DC.

Simons, Thomas W. 1998b. Bad News for Pak Afghan Policy: GOP Support for the Taliban Appears to Be Getting Stronger [from US Embassy Islamabad to Secretary of State Albright]. 1 July 1998. US Department of State, document accessed at the National Security Archive, Washington, DC.

Smyth, William Henry. 1994. New Fighting and New Forces in Kandahar [from US Consulate Peshawar to Secretary of State Christopher]. 3 November 1994. US Department of State, document accessed at the National Security Archive, Washington, DC.

CHAPTER 3

The Taliban Take Kabul and a New Friend Moves to Kandahar

Abstract The Taliban took Kabul on 17 September 1996 and had a legitimate claim to be the government of Afghanistan. The Taliban wanted a good relationship with the United States for many reasons including fear of Iran and Russia. The US and the Taliban met regularly in Afghanistan, Pakistan, and the US. On 8 November 1996, the Taliban formally requested diplomatic recognition from the United States. Washington had four major concerns regarding Afghanistan: stability and ending the Taliban/Northern Alliance conflict; drug trafficking; women's rights; and the presence of Osama bin Laden and his Al Qaeda terrorist network. This chapter looks at the discussions and high-level meetings between the United States and the Taliban from the fall of Kabul until the 7 August 1998 Al Qaeda attacks in Kenya and Tanzania—a time period during which concern about both women's rights and terrorism grew dramatically.

Keywords Afghanistan · Diplomatic history · Osama bin Laden
Taliban · United Nations · United States foreign policy

The Taliban took Kabul on 17 September 1996. They now had a legitimate claim as the government of Afghanistan. In a meeting at the American embassy in Islamabad, Taliban Deputy Foreign Affairs Advisor Abdul Jalil told his American hosts that the official name of the new government was the "Afghan Taliban Government" and said that

© The Author(s) 2019

J. Cristol, *The United States and the Taliban before and after 9/11*,
https://doi.org/10.1007/978-3-319-97172-8_3

Kabul would remain the administrative capital of Afghanistan, but that Kandahar would serve as the capital of the Taliban movement (Simons 1996a). The Taliban took every opportunity to voice their fond feelings about the United States. The US had supported Afghanistan in its struggle against the Soviet Union only seven years earlier, and there was plenty of goodwill. Former Secretary of State Madeline Albright wrote in her 2005 (p. 461) memoir that, "In those years, Taliban leaders didn't express hostility towards America; in fact they thanked the United States for its role in ousting the Soviets." The Taliban never overtly nor covertly turned on the United States, but their naivety and intransigence, combined with Mullah Omar's growing relationship with Osama bin Laden, who had returned to Afghanistan and opened a series of terrorist training camps near the Afghan city Khost, would eventually make a good relationship impossible.

The CIA's 30 September 1996 "National Intelligence Daily" provides an analysis of the Taliban's victory. In its discussion of the Taliban political leadership, the still-classified author writes, "US officials who have met with Taliban leaders have been struck by their lack of sophistication and ignorance of administrative processes." They have "no discernible economic policy beyond Koranic injunctions against usury" and they have not closed "camps associated with Osama bin Laden." The report was not entirely pessimistic about US/Taliban relations, saying that there was "no evidence that a Taliban government would be systematically unfriendly to US interests" (Deutch 1996).

The subject of recognition was also discussed in the report. Pakistan was thought to be close to recognizing the Taliban government, but was concerned about Iran's reaction, and the author noted that the Taliban government would soon want the US to recognize it as well. Ultimately, the CIA author's opinion was prescient. They believed that, "Dialogue likely [would] founder on profound differences" and the Taliban's "willingness to risk losing aid from international organizations over its treatment of women hints at the group's inflexibility" (Deutch 1996). Pulitzer Prize-winning journalist Roy Gutman (2008, p. 125) writes that, "Omar's messianic worldview was built around the fatwas of sympathetic religious scholars and had no room for political compromise." The US did not realize just how inflexible he would be, perhaps because, for now, there were good reasons to work together.

It was not only latent affection that made the Taliban favorably disposed toward closer relations with the United States but the Taliban also feared both Russia and Iran. Steve Coll, in his Pulitzer Prize-winning book *Ghost Wars* (2004, pp. 336–340), writes that the Taliban "fully expected to end up in a war with Iran." The Taliban turned down a CIA offer of between $5–8 million for their 53 stinger missiles as they anticipated needing them in that war (Coll 2004, pp. 336–340).

The Taliban had good reason to fear Iran. In their takeover of the city Mazar-i-Sharif, the Taliban murdered between 9 and 11 Iranian diplomats (reliable sources differ on the exact number), who they claim aided the Northern Alliance in the region. Regardless of the accuracy of that claim, the murder was a clear and direct violation of the 1961 Vienna Convention on Diplomatic Relations.[1] In late August 1999, a truck bomb went off outside Omar's home. The bomb killed two of his brothers and his brother-in-law (Gutman 2008, p. 186). The Taliban suspected that Iranian agents planted the bomb in retaliation for the incident in Mazar-i-Sharif (Gannon 2005, p. 76). Taliban Deputy Foreign Affairs Advisor Abdul Jalil voiced his concern that Iran, "harbors several thousand anti-Taliban Afghans, who it may use to invade" (Simons 1996a). Taliban concerns were at least partially validated when Iran amassed 70,000 troops on the Iran/Afghanistan border.

Iran had worries of its own. Tehran was concerned that the Taliban was "part of the US plan to encircle and isolate Iran" (Rubin 1998, par. 66). In testimony before the Senate Foreign Relations Committee, then Council on Foreign Relations Afghanistan expert Barnett Rubin (1998, par. 2) said that, "War, or at least military action [between Iran and the Taliban], cannot be ruled out." Iran was also concerned that the Taliban would allow the Mujahedeen-e-Khalq terrorist group to operate from its territory.[2]

The Taliban victory in Kabul was quickly followed by victories that led to their control of 90% of Afghan territory. The US needed to figure out a response to this new reality in Kabul. Washington moved to increase contacts with the new Taliban government and to work with them on issues of mutual (and of course American) interest. Secretary of State Warren Christopher sent instructions to US Ambassador to Pakistan Thomas W. Simons in Islamabad. He authorized Simons to send representatives to meet with the Taliban in Kabul and to "demonstrate [Washington's] willingness to deal with them as the new authorities in Kabul." The US diplomats said that they hoped, "[The Taliban would] propose soon an envoy to represent [its] government in Washington" and that the State Department would decline to renew visas for the existing, non-Taliban, Afghan diplomats in the United States. Washington was also willing to reopen its embassy in Kabul, closed since 1979, "Subject to security concerns" (Christopher 1996a).

The US did not ultimately reopen its embassy in Kabul until the fall of the Taliban in 2002. However, it is important to note that if the US had reopened its embassy, that action would not have constituted recognition of the Taliban government. Diplomatic recognition is not the same as the opening of diplomatic relations. Even the use of the term "interim government" or the phrase "we recognize that the Taliban now control Kabul and much of the country," does not construe de facto recognition of the Taliban government. The United States does not recognize the concept of "de facto recognition."[3]

Christopher (1996a) told Ambassador Simons that special emphasis should be put on the historic friendship between the US and Afghanistan—"The United States has had a long history of friendship with the Afghan people, and we look forward to a future of the same." The overall tone Christopher wished to convey to the Taliban was one of friendship and cooperation. There was no difference between the public and private tone of the State Department toward the Taliban.

In multiple press conferences, State Department spokesmen Nicolas Burns and Glyn Davies voiced the Clinton Administration's willingness to work with the Taliban. Davies (1996a) said that the administration "hope[s] that [the Taliban takeover of Kabul] presents an opportunity for a process of national reconciliation to begin." The hope the administration had for the Taliban was so high that when asked, "This group— this Islamic fundamentalist group that has taken Afghanistan by force and summarily executed the former President, the United States is holding out on the possibility of relations?" Davies (1996b) responded, "I'm not going to prejudge where we're going to go with Afghanistan.... It's clear that the Taliban are in charge of Kabul.... Our call on them is to use their new position to move to a process of national reconciliation." State Department responses to questions about the relationship with the Taliban scarcely deviated from this line throughout this period.

The United States might have been hopeful about the Taliban and desired good relations, but there were four major issues standing in the way both of American recognition of the Taliban government and of a normal relationship: ending the ongoing conflict between the Taliban and the Northern Alliance and returning stability to Afghanistan; the opium trade; human rights, especially the rights of women and girls;

and terrorism, especially the presence of Al Qaeda leader Osama bin Laden. Secretary Christopher (1996a) told Ambassador Simons to ask the Taliban if they "know the location of ex-Saudi financier and radical Islamist Osama bin Laden.... His continued presence here would not, we believe, serve Afghanistan's interests." There is no indication that any American official yet understood how obstinate the Taliban would be about these issues.

The United States brought up women's rights in the regular meetings between Taliban and American officials. Nicolas Burns said in a press conference that the US "press[ed]... for women's rights" in its regular meetings with the Taliban. However, the US was hesitant to issue any public condemnations of the Taliban, saying that generally the US cares about such things and that specifically "we will need to assess what happens in Kabul" (Burns 1996). There was hope that the US could forge a good relationship with the Taliban and thus be in a better position to moderate their practices, if not their actual views. The US was not unique in this regard; the United Nations did not take a forceful public position against the Taliban's treatment of woman either.[4] Associated Press reporter Kathy Gannon (2005, p. 47) writes that the Taliban, "were actually seen as a good thing in that they were expected to put an end to the brutal fighting and lawlessness, and bring security to a deeply insecure nation." The primary documents support her assertion.

Before the Taliban captured Kabul, there was no international reaction to their restrictive measures against women. Gannon (2005, p. 47) writes that, "The Taliban were consistent, and from the very beginning, there could be no mistake about their attitude toward women. But the international community didn't care." Gannon (2005, p. 47) rightly points out that women did not do well under the previous government. However, the situation was much worse under the Taliban. The Taliban's treatment of women is "arguably the worst in all recorded history" (Schulz and Schulz 1999, p. 237). The Taliban were educated only in Arabic translations of the Koran, a language they did not understand and thus they were highly suggestible to the ideas put forward by their teachers. The Taliban forbade virtually everything, from board games to phones to cameras. Women were effectively barred from leaving the house except with a male relative. The windows of houses with women living in them were required to paint the windows black. When women did leave the home, they were required to be covered from head to toe in burqas. The burqa itself could cost up to three months of the average wage (Schulz and Schulz 1999, p. 243).

As the Taliban consolidated power in Afghanistan and made their first bid to be recognized as that country's legitimate government, their treatment of women and girls began to gather attention in the United States and internationally. US Permanent Representative to the United Nations Madeline Albright spoke at a private home to the Women's Foreign Policy Group on 19 November 1996. In her speech, she said that, "In Afghanistan a rebel force called the Taliban has seized control of half the country. Along the way it has issued decrees that would essentially deprive women of all rights, except the right to remain silent, indoors. Uneducated and invisible.... Women and girls are being denied the chance to work, to go to school and to participate freely in the day to day life of their communities. The Taliban's great claim is that the harshness of their rule creates stability and diminishes crime.... The rule of law depends not on terror, but on respect between the governors and the governed, and the future of Afghanistan will indeed be grim.... That is why the UN Security Council voted last month, with strong United States support, to condemn the Taliban's egregious violations of human rights and to urge a moderation of its policies" (Albright 1996, pp. 21–24). This resolution, UNSCR 1076, "denounce[d] the discrimination against girls and women and other violations of human rights and international humanitarian law in Afghanistan."

In what was likely a deliberate choice of words, Albright referred to the Taliban as a "rebel group," which explicitly meant that they could not yet be recognized as Afghanistan's legitimate government. Moreover, it would be legal under international law to assist the recognized government in its attempt to suppress the rebellion. UNSCR 1076 did not go that far, and called on all states not to supply arms to any side nor interfere in "the internal affairs of Afghanistan."

Women's rights was an important issue for the American public, but for the State Department, Defense Department, and intelligence community, the presence of Osama bin Laden was clearly the most important issue in US/Taliban relations. On 28 September 1996, the day after the Taliban took Bagram Air Base, Jalil had an hour-long conversation with the political officer at the US Embassy in Islamabad. Jalil told his American interlocutor that Osama bin Laden was not in Taliban territory (Simons 1996a). That was true. Bin Laden was not invited to Afghanistan by the Taliban, nor had he met them during the jihad against the Soviet Union.

Osama bin Laden was expelled by Sudan and moved to Afghanistan on 19 May 1996 as the guest of a local warlord named Yunis Khalis (Filkins 2001, par. 51).[5] The *New York Times* reported that he was first introduced to the Taliban by Pakistan's Inter-Services Intelligence (ISI) and that bin Laden gave the Taliban an initial $3 million donation (LeVine and Bonner 1998, p. A6). Bin Laden did not yet live in Taliban-controlled territory and US diplomats had probably spent more time with Taliban officials than had bin Laden.

The United States moved quickly to meet with the new rulers of Kabul. Deputy Foreign Minister Jalil visited Ambassador Simons' Islamabad home on 7 October 1996. Jalil was there to deliver a personal message from Mullah Omar. He said that the Taliban thought highly of the United States and appreciated the help in the jihad against the Soviets, but, for domestic reasons, Omar asked that the relationship with the United States be kept "quiet and low key" (Simons 1996b). Afghanistan's Shia population believed that the Taliban was created by the US, so Omar thought it best if the United Arab Emirates (UAE) and Saudi Arabia were the first countries to recognize the Taliban government.[6] Jalil suggested that, "Acting Foreign Minister" Mullah Mohammed Ghaus, who had visited the US just a few months earlier, could meet with Simons at the embassy rather than at Simons' home. This would make the meeting more official. Simons delivered his talking points. He told Jalil that the US wanted a broad-based government in Afghanistan and that Washington was "deeply concerned [about] due process and respect for basic human rights, especially relating to women" (Simons 1996b). Moreover, the Taliban's treatment of women may impact their access to international aid. The conversation went well and Simons (1996b) noted in his report that the Taliban "may be more politically sophisticated than generally acknowledged." Events would prove that they were not. Simons had planned to visit Kabul, Mazar-i-Sharif, and Kandahar, but the Taliban put the visit on hold until after the UAE and Saudi Arabia recognized the Taliban (Simons 1996c).

By mid-October, the Taliban consolidated their gains over most of the country, but a 1996 report by Canada's International Advisory Committee (IAC) claimed that they did not meet the standard of "effective control" necessary for recognition: "To achieve effective control throughout Afghanistan, [the] Taliban still must co-opt or neutralize the military strongmen in the North." The IAC wrote that, "Taliban leaders will have to focus on ... obtaining international recognition as the de facto government.... their main argument will be that as they exercise effective control over the government machinery, they can bring law and order and a degree of stability to the country not experienced for several years." TheIAC did not believe that the UN would seat the Taliban either, writing that, "The UN credentials committee... is unlikely to consider any application by Taliban for a change in representation." And if that wasn't harsh enough, an unnamed Canadian government source said that the "Taliban does not have a clear grasp of the UN System or of what the UN stands for in terms of values" ("IAC Intelligence Assessment" 1996). This assessment was accurate.

The Taliban talked about recognition, but did not formally request recognition from the United States until an 8 November 1996 meeting between Ambassador Simons and Acting Foreign Minister Ghaus. Ghaus was joined by Acting Reconstruction Minister Attiqullah, and Afghan Embassy Chargé d'Affairs Abdul Wahab; Simons was joined by two others.[7] Ghaus voiced the Taliban's strong desire for good relations with the United States both because the US was a former ally in the war against the USSR and because they perceived Russia and Iran to be the biggest strategic threats to the Taliban.[8] He then made the case for recognition: "A government that controls a country's territory is the legitimate government. Thus, the Taliban, which control over two-thirds of the country, should be recognized as the Afghan government." This case was reasonable in theory, though two-thirds would be a low standard for "effective control." Simons replied by praising the Afghan people: "We admired the Afghans' freedom struggle, and were proud of our role in its success." He had hoped that after the war against the Soviets, the Afghans would come together, but unfortunately they continued fighting. Ghaus blamed the ongoing civil war on "interference by Russia, Iran, and India" (Simons 1996d).

This meeting may have been the first extended dialogue about Osama bin Laden between the US and the Taliban. Simons asked Ghaus about Osama bin Laden and told him that the US "received reports that he is in or near the Taliban-controlled city of Jalalabad" and that, "we hope he is not there with Taliban acquiescence." Ghaus assured Simons that bin Laden was not in a Taliban-controlled area; but in his post-conversation notes, Simons wrote that there is a "body of evidence increasingly tilting toward the conclusion that the Taliban are not being totally candid" (1996e). It is also possible that they did not know.

Simons said that the US position on the end of the conflict was that there should be a "genuine negotiation of a political settlement which respected the rights of all Afghans, including minorities and women." Ghaus, betraying a lack of understanding of democracy, voiced his preference for a Northern Alliance surrender because, "In democracies minorities must always submit to the will of the majority" and he believed that the ethnically Pashtun Taliban comprised the majority of Afghanistan's population. Ghaus ended the meeting by saying, "We want the United States government to recognize the Taliban's interim government" and that after the Taliban victory, we hope to "have reason to be grateful to the United States for its help." Ghaus asked to send a delegation to the United States and said that any US delegations would be welcome in Afghanistan. Simons reported the tone of the meeting as "courteous and civil" (Simons 1996d).

The US continued to try to make inroads with the Taliban on the subjects of women's rights and the presence of Osama bin Laden. On 10 December 1996, two meetings were held in Pakistan between the United States and the Taliban. A still-classified source met with Assistant Secretary of State for South Asian Affairs Robin Raphel, Afghanistan Desk Officer R.L. Chew, State Department South Asia expert Lee Coldren, and a still-classified American. In both meetings, the Americans brought up the Taliban's treatment of women and pointed out that, "Women not working could lead to starvation for families" (Christopher 1996b).

Recognition was another topic of discussion at the meeting. The Americans asked about the structure of the Taliban government and said that there was a simple administration in place, but no bureaucracy and an "oral rather than written code." Raphel replied that that was, "Not enough to constitute a government" (Christopher 1996b). The Taliban representative said that they would not seek the UN seat just yet, and a still-classified source pointed out that they had "major obstacles in gaining international recognition" (Christopher 1996b). It was true that the Taliban faced obstacles in gaining recognition, but those obstacles were due to the result of recognition's political nature more than due to the United Nations criteria for recognition of governments. The Taliban had at least as good a claim on recognition as does the government of Somalia, which controls only 73% of Somalia's territory. The source described the Taliban as divided between the *mujahedeen*, who were worldly but had little influence, and the more influential madrasa students with ties to Pakistan (Christopher 1996b). Other new Taliban cared more about politics than they did religion or jihad.

Perhaps the greatest obstacle to the Taliban's effort to be recognized was the nomination of UN Ambassador Albright to be the new Secretary of State on 6 December 1996. She had been vociferous in her denunciations of the Taliban and now would oversee America's relationship with the "rebel group." In Secretary Christopher's "lame duck" period, a flurry of meetings between the US and the Taliban took place.

US Deputy Chief of Mission in Islamabad John Holzman traveled to Afghanistan for three days of meetings. On 5 January, he met with Jalil and on 6 January, he met with Jalil, Deputy Foreign Minister Sher Mohammad Abbas Stanakzai and Mullah Mohammed Rabbani. Rabbani was the only Taliban leader with a large power base independent of Mullah Omar (Simons 1997h) and he was generally more moderate in his positions and his tone. Rabbani was the Taliban's second-in-command and held the official positions of Governor of Kandahar and Head of the Council of Ministers. It was at these meetings that the Taliban first acknowledged that Osama bin Laden was their "guest." They were keen to explain to Holzman that they did not support terrorism and told him that, "[bin Laden] has been asked not to carry out terrorist activities against other countries" (Hanson 1997). They took a similar approach to terrorist training camps. These could remain open and the people there could stay in them as "refugees," but they "could not engage in hostilities" (Hanson 1997).

Rabbani and Stanakzai reiterated this point on 6 January.[9] In response, Holzman pointed out that bin Laden was plotting against the Saudis, who are "friends of the Taliban" (Hanson 1997). Rabbani replied that bin Laden was "a refugee." They had spoken to him and asked him not to carry out terrorist activities to which he agreed. Holzman told them that the US had information that bin Laden was indeed plotting terrorist activities. Rabbani reminded him that bin Laden promised that he would not do so. The almost-comical back-and-forth would be repeated in slow motion over the following years. And just in case Holzman did not get the message, a still-classified Taliban source met with Simons on 6 February and told him that the Taliban, "Won't allow our territory to be used by Osama bin Laden for [terrorism]" (Simons 1997c).

Perhaps in an effort to reassure his American guests, Jalil said that bin Laden had been living in caves in Tora Bora, but the Taliban were suspicious about his activities. So, in order to keep a close eye on him, they told him he had to live "in an ordinary house" (Hanson 1997). Rabbani expressed what would become a long-standing Taliban position—what Osama bin Laden did in the past was not their concern, the Taliban would have no issue with bin Laden unless he did something new. Holzman let his hosts know that the association with bin Laden was hurting the Taliban and that they "do not owe [him] anything" (Hanson 1997). Osama bin Laden's move from Tora Bora to Kandahar was not for America's benefit, and it served to draw Mullah Omar and Osama bin Laden closer together. Bin Laden showered largess on his new friends, building "a grand mosque... and constructing key roads" (Rashid 2009, p. 15). The two met regularly and even became fishing buddies (Wright 2007, p. 326).

The next day, at a meeting in Kabul with Acting Head of the Interim Shura (and future foreign minister) Mullah Mohammed Hassan, Holzman heard another of what would become a standard Taliban talking point. "The Taliban cannot expel [bin Laden]," Hassan told Holzman, citing the tribal code of Pashtunwali that governs the treatment of guests in Pashtun culture.[10]

Holzman concluded that, "The Taliban appear to have concluded that it is in their interest to give [bin Laden] refuge." It was possible bin Laden was paying off "some individual Taliban" and "how hard they may have pressed him not to commit terrorist acts is unknown." Holzman suggested to Washington that the US "urge Saudi and Egyptian authorities to take a more active approach with the Taliban on bin Laden" (Hanson 1997). Though his Taliban hosts told Holzman that US authorities could inspect the terrorist training camps, those visits were repeatedly delayed by the Taliban.

After Holzman's trip to Afghanistan, the US embassy in Islamabad began planning for Secretary of State Madeline Albright's first trip to Islamabad. In his "scene-setter," for the new Secretary, Holzman recapped his recent trips to Afghanistan. He reported that things seemed to be going reasonably well in Taliban-controlled areas, "Markets are full by Afghan standards.... [and] small pharmacies... are well stocked with mostly Pakistani drugs." The quality of life had become better in Kandahar since the Taliban took over. Holzman reported that, "Life is not so bad and the people of Kandahar would be crazy not to prefer

Taliban theocracy to factional warfare." But Kandahar was a conservative city anyway, and the Taliban's light touch in Kandahar might have been the result of the need not to alienate their base of support. In Kabul and Herat, the Taliban's rule was "harsh and oppressive" and getting worse. There was already a backlash in Kabul and Mullah Omar took steps "to create a kinder, gentler occupation," cracking down on Taliban beating people for non-conformity (Simons 1997b).

Holzman also brought up the recognition issue, writing to Albright that, "We've also heard bucketsful from the Taliban that they, as the rulers of Kabul, haven't been recognized as Afghanistan's government" (Simons 1997b). They were especially upset that the UN Credentials Committee refused to seat them. Holzman was concerned that the Taliban were becoming disillusioned with the West and that the more radical members of the Taliban were gaining power (Simons 1997b). Filkins (2008, p. 29) wrote, "More than anything, what served to bother the Taliban leaders… was the refusal of the United Nations to extend them formal recognition even though they'd conquered 90% of the country."

In the United States, concern for Afghanistan's women grew and the issue was becoming a cause célèbre among celebs. In Washington, Connecticut Senator Christopher Dodd, who would later become the chairman of the Motion Picture Association of America, introduced a resolution on 7 February that expressed "concern for the deterioration of human rights in Afghanistan" and emphasized "the need for a peaceful political settlement" (1997). The resolution said that Congress was "disturbed" by the restrictions the Taliban placed on women. It "deplored" the Taliban's human rights violations and "condemned" the discrimination against women and girls. It called on US President Bill Clinton to "call for an end to discrimination against women and girls in Afghanistan" and to ask Pakistan to do what it could to change the Taliban's gender policies.[11]

Two months after Holzman's trip to Kandahar and Kabul, an even more senior-level visit took place. State Department Deputy Director for Pakistan/Afghanistan/Bangladesh (PAB) Donald A. Camp traveled to Kandahar and Kabul with Brad Hanson and the embassy's political counselor for a series of meetings on 2–3 March 1997. On 2 March in Kabul, Camp met with Ghaus and Afghanistan Bank Chairman Mullah Ehsanullah Ehsan.[12] On 3 March, he met with Stanakzai in Kandahar. The subject of these meetings was Osama bin Laden. Ehsan reminded

Camp that bin Laden had originally been invited to Afghanistan by ene-
mies of the Taliban. He assured the Americans that bin Laden couldn't
communicate with his followers, and that the Taliban didn't know
exactly where he is. Stanakzai further downplayed the relationship and
said that the Taliban were not taking money from bin Laden, in fact, he
"was being fed by the Taliban." This contradicted the earlier meeting in
which it was suggested that bin Laden was forced from Tora Bora pre-
cisely so that the Taliban could keep an eye on him; and it contradicted
Ehsan's statement that the Taliban did not know where he was. In many
instances, it is unclear if the Taliban were lying to the Americans or were
genuinely unable to keep tabs on Osama bin Laden. Ambassador Simons
(1997d) noted in his post-trip memo that Ehsan, "Seemed to want to
bargain Taliban action against bin Laden for US action on recognition of
the Taliban government." This may be the first instance of the possibility
of the US trading recognition for bin Laden.

The official record indicates that Stanakzai's statement about bin
Laden was not true. In fact, just a few months later the CIA referred
to "large amounts of money bin Laden is spending on support for the
Taliban" ("DCI Talking Points" 1997). It could be that Stanakzai was
downplaying the relationship to indicate that the Taliban was willing to
give up bin Laden for the right "price."

The United States was well-aware that the Taliban were not good
faith negotiators. Ambassador Simons suggested to Raphel that she tell
Congress that US policy should be to "simultaneously engage with the
Taliban and criticize their abuses." The hope was that the Taliban could
be moderated. That hope was not entirely unreasonable. The extent of
Mullah Omar's intransigence was not yet known, and the US attempted
to figure out what sort of pressure or inducements could be used to get
the desired results from the Taliban. Simons (1997e) also suggested that
Raphel propose an "Afghanistan Reconstruction Escrow Fund" as an
incentive for a negotiated settlement with the Northern Alliance.

Though Osama bin Laden had not yet perpetrated any of his most
famous attacks against American targets, the US intelligence community
was becoming increasingly worried about bin Laden. In March 1997,
the US gained intelligence that bin Laden was attempting to acquire ura-
nium and was, "exploring the possibility of mounting operations with
weapons of mass destruction" ("Osama bin Laden's Attempts" 1997).
This made him a much higher priority than he had ever been before and
the need to pressure the Taliban to expel bin Laden had never been direr.

The United States continued to push for a solution to the outstanding issues with the Taliban in the UN Security Council, where it took a diplomatic approach to the problem. On 14 April 1997, US Deputy Permanent Representative to the United Nations Edward "Skip" Gnehm said that the, "United States Government has repeatedly urged an end to the fighting and urged a practical dialogue in the spirit of compromise.... Stability cannot be achieved if one group tries to rule Afghanistan on its own." In response to accusations that the US supported the Taliban, he replied, "We do not support the Taliban or any other group. But neither do we put blame on the Taliban for the ills of Afghanistan." He informed the UNSC that the US' chief concerns in Afghanistan were terrorist training camps, opium, and the rights of women and girls. Gnehm (1997) pointed out that while "much of the populace has accepted Taliban rule," that is because they have brought "a modicum of peace to Afghanistan," not because they favor their restrictive policies.

Soon after, Gnehm's boss, US Permanent Representative to the United Nations Bill Richardson, traveled with the new Assistant Secretary of State for South Asia, Karl Inderfurth, to Afghanistan to meet with Mohammed Rabbani. This was the first cabinet-level visit to Afghanistan in 24 years. Richardson arrived on 17 April and was "deluged with gifts of saddlebags and turbans. He was also invited to watch a game of polo played in traditional fashion with the headless carcass of a sheep" (Rashid 1998, par. 2). He was there to express support for a peace accord between the Taliban and the Northern Alliance. Richardson also asked that women be allowed to return to the jobs from which they were barred when the Taliban took over. The Taliban "agreed" to rethink its approach to women's higher education and to their treatment of UN aid workers, though no changes were ultimately made (Rashid 1998, par. 9). But those were not the only reasons he was there. As *The Economist* noted, he did not go to Kabul "mainly to plead for women's rights.... He hinted that possible recognition of the Kabul government was on America's mind if there were genuine progress towards a peace settlement" ("Those not very nice" 1998, p. 41). Richardson successfully persuaded the Northern Alliance and the Taliban to hold talks, but the talks soon broke down and ultimately Richardson's visit yielded no practical results.

The Taliban achieved a series of major victories on a single day—26 May 1997. They tightened their grip on the country when they took control of Mazar-i-Sharif. John Burns (1997, par. 4) wrote in the

New York Times that, "No government has had similar authority since 1978." The Taliban had achieved "effective control" over 90% of the country. Pakistani policy was to recognize whoever was in power in Kabul, but it had waited until the fall of Mazar-i-Sharif to act (Simons 1997f). Soon after the city's capture, Pakistan became the first country to recognize the Taliban as the legitimate government of Afghanistan. Pakistani Foreign Minister Gohar Ayub Khan announced Pakistan's belief that, "all others should follow suit" (Rubin 1998, par. 54). Sure enough, Saudi and Emirati recognition soon followed. The Taliban, according to Simons (1997e), were "widely believed to be in some sort of 'special relationship'" with the Saudis, and had long enjoyed the support of the Pakistani intelligence service. However, Pakistan's policy toward the UN seat was that it should be vacant (Simons 1997g).

The victories of that day were quickly marred by two events. First, the ransacking of the Iranian consulate in Mazar-i-Sharif and the murder of Iran's diplomats effectively destroyed whatever potential remained for a working relationship between Iran and the Taliban. On the floor of the United Nations General Assembly, the United States condemned the murders of the Iranian diplomats and called for an investigation (Burleigh 1998). Second, there was a shake up at the State Department and, "The entire chain of command on Afghanistan... all retired or were reassigned in the summer of 1997... The new team brought with it a new outlook and a new vocabulary. What had once been vague references to international 'misgivings' about the Taliban's human rights violations became unapologetic condemnations" (Mackenzie 1998, p. 101). To make matters worse, they promptly lost control of the city again.

The Taliban's latest victories (and defeats) also attracted more international attention and American condemnation. On 23 September 1997, New York Congresswoman Carolyn Maloney submitted a concurrent resolution expressing Congress' concern about the situation in Afghanistan. This resolution focused on the treatment of women and girls, but also mentioned drug proliferation and terrorist training camps. The substance was similar to an earlier resolution Maloney had submitted, co-sponsored by Christopher Dodd, though it was now joined by 24 other Congressmen. Awareness of the Taliban in the halls of Congress was growing.

The US held another high-level meeting with the Taliban on 8 December 1997. This time, the meeting was different for three major reasons. First, it was held in the US. Second, it took place under the direct order of Mullah Omar. Third, it was held "under the auspices of

Unocal," the American oil company that hoped to build a pipeline from Turkmenistan through Afghanistan to Pakistan. The US team was led by Inderfurth and attended by PAB Office Director, Michael Malinowski, and the Afghanistan Desk Officers. The Taliban were represented by Acting Minister for Mines and Industry Armad Jin, Acting Minister for Information and Culture Amir Khan Mottaqi, Acting Minister for Planning Din Mohammed Mujahid, and Din's brother-in-law Mujahid, the Taliban's Permanent-Representative to the UN designate. The Taliban had a few goals in mind for the meeting including "improved relations with the US"; the reopening of the US embassy in Kabul; and crop substitution assistance (Talbott 1997). The Taliban delegation was also eager to see Unocal's pipeline move forward. The United States was interested in talking about women's rights. The US and the Taliban were now meeting regularly, and having cordial, diplomatic discussions; but they were having two different conversations.

Mottaqi was "more extreme on social issues than most Taliban" (Simons 1997h). He did most of the talking for the Taliban and warned that they would be "overthrown" if they altered their requirement for the veiling of women. He said that they had no desire to "stop female education" and pointed out that the US had never had a female president. Inderfurth responded that, "Our attitude toward the Taliban would be influenced by its behavior relating to medical care, education, and opportunities for women." Mottaqi replied that Afghanistan was not a "normal country" and there had never been much female education (Talbott 1997).

On the subject of recognition, Inderfurth said that the Taliban could not be the only player in the government "and receive US recognition." Inderfurth had to leave the meeting early and Malinowski took the lead for the United States. Malinowski asked for a reaffirmation of the Taliban's commitment that Osama bin Laden would not use Afghanistan as a base for attacks, and Mottaqi reaffirmed this commitment. Din Mohammed chimed in and said that if bin Laden were expelled, he would go to Iran "and cause more trouble" (Talbott 1997). This represented a new argument for the Taliban—that they were doing the United States a favor by providing sanctuary for Osama bin Laden. They consistently argued that he would cause more harm outside of Afghanistan than he could from inside Afghanistan. Armad Jin said that they had stopped Iran and Iraq from contacting bin Laden and stopped him from giving public interviews. Jin raised the pipeline issue and said that both the Taliban and Pakistan would like to proceed with a pipeline. Malinowski said that while the US favored a pipeline too, there needed to be peace first.

The Taliban expressed gratitude for the material and moral support the US provided Afghanistan in the war against the USSR, but their list of requests was long. They wanted friendly relations with the US based on "mutual respect and non-interference." They wanted funding to rebuild boys' and girls' schools. They wanted help bringing the culprits of massacres of Taliban POWs to justice. They wanted help stopping Iranian arms shipments to Bamiyan and Mazar-i-Sharif. And they wanted the US to reopen its embassy in Kabul, which "will... help open up a vista of cooperation on wide-ranging matters between the two friendly countries and peoples." The US delegation noted that the Taliban's "concern over their image in the US came through" (Talbott 1997).

Shortly thereafter, Holzman left Islamabad to become the new US Ambassador to Bangladesh. His replacement, Alan Eastham, arrived from New Delhi, where he had been the embassy's political counselor, and got off to a busy start. He met with Taliban Ambassador to Pakistan Shahabuddin Dilawar and then visited Kabul, where he met with Acting Interior Minister Kharullah Kharkhwah (Simons 1998a). As concern about Osama bin Laden grew, the US continued to explore the possibility of a split within the Taliban. The primary focus was on Deputy Leader Rabbani, who had the support of many Taliban leaders. However, a source told the US embassy in Islamabad that Rabbani was not necessarily a moderate and that he "wholeheartedly supports... Omar's policies on gender issues and on providing a safe haven to Saudi terrorist financier Osama bin Laden" (Eastham 1997). The source was likely correct about Rabbani's views on gender issues, but it would become clear as the months passed that Rabbani and Omar's views of bin Laden differed.

Even though there were friendly meetings happening behind the scenes, President Bill Clinton continued to publicly denounce the Taliban and their treatment of women. On 11 March 1998, International Women's Day, Clinton spoke in the East Room of the White House to an audience that included Secretary-General Kofi Annan. Though his verbal remarks only briefly mentioned the Taliban, the White House statement devoted one-third of its text to the issue of women in Afghanistan. It said, "The United States has repeatedly condemned Taliban human rights violations, particularly against women and girls" ("President Clinton: A Historic" 1998).

These human rights violations were brought up in a 2 July 1998 meeting between the United States and the Taliban. Political Counselor Joe Novak met with a still-classified member of the Taliban. Novak asked that the closure of home-based schools for girls, and the requirement that a close male relative accompany a female for medical treatment be rescinded. The unnamed Talib was "obviously uncomfortable" with the requests. He argued that the schools were closed because they were unregistered and the international community had not built enough gender-segregated schools. On the subject of bin Laden, Novak pointed out that while the Taliban had assured the US that bin Laden would not be allowed to talk to the press, he had made public threats against the United States in May and July. The Talib replied that bin Laden was now "under control in Kandahar" and promised that he would now "fully submit" to the Taliban's requests. This foreshadowed another trend in US/Taliban relations: The Taliban would assure the US that bin Laden was under control, bin Laden would prove the Taliban wrong, and the Taliban would assure the US that he was, finally, under control. The Talib also told Novak that their representative in New York, Abdul Wahab, who was unpopular and spoke little English, would likely be replaced with Stanakzai (Simons 1998c). Wahab was reassigned from New York to Riyadh, but was ultimately replaced by Abdul Hakim Mujahid, who was reassigned to New York from Pakistan. Omar frequently reassigned personnel, possibly to prevent anyone from building too strong of an independent power base (Simons 1997a).

Later that month, Inderfurth and Eastham met with Pakistani Foreign Minister Shamshad Ahmed. At the same time, Minister of Higher Education Mullah Hamdullah Nomani was in the United States to raise money for women's universities and girls' schools. Inderfurth said that the Taliban's behavior toward women was "impossible to explain since most Islamic states do not act like they do." Ahmed's reply pivoted away from gender issues and back to recognition: "The Taliban are angered that they are not recognized by the international community and blame the United Nations" (Simons 1998d). Barnett Rubin (1998, par. 13) backs up this account. In his Congressional Testimony, he points out that, "The Taliban resent the fact that although they have provided security for UN and NGO staff and property, the opposition, which has failed to do so, continues to be recognized as the government of Afghanistan by most countries and to occupy Afghanistan's UN seat." The meeting with Ahmed took place at a time of increasing Pakistani support for the Taliban (Simons 1998b).

The US' attempts to secure bin Laden were not limited to a seemingly endless series of meetings with Taliban officials. The CIA was making plans to snatch him from Afghanistan. By May, a "full rendition operation was designed, practiced... and ready to go" ("Talking Points Regarding Osama" 1998). Unfortunately, their teams were never close enough, and victory was not likely enough, to get the green light from the Clinton Administration. Then, on 7 August 1998, Al Qaeda attacked the US embassies in Kenya and Tanzania, killing over 200 people. Bin Laden went from the obsession of a small team at the CIA, and the grave concern of American diplomats in Pakistan and elsewhere, to global public enemy number one. This made the Taliban a target, but also gave them a tremendous amount of leverage. The Taliban were in a position to extract concessions from the US for turning over bin Laden; and no matter how much Lionel Ritchie might disapprove, the US would likely have made those concessions. But the US/Taliban relationship was cordially sliding toward oblivion.

NOTES

1. That the Taliban were not the recognized government did not absolve them of their obligations under the Vienna Convention.
2. The Mujahedeen-e-Khalq are an Iranian exile group who fought with Saddam Hussein against Iran in the Iran/Iraq War. They were on the US State Department's list of Foreign Terrorist Organizations until 2012.
3. Former assistant legal advisor to the US State Department, Marjorie Whiteman, wrote that, "In prevailing practice, when the United States extends recognition, it is recognition per se not 'de facto' recognition" (quoted in Cochran 1968, p. 457). After some confusion about the use of the word "per se," she issued a clarification that "per se" meant "de jure" (Cochran 1968, p. 457).
4. For a somewhat shocking discussion of this issue see Gannon (2005, Chapter 3).
5. The Taliban claimed that he was originally invited by former prime minister Gulbuddin Hekmatyar (Simons 1996e), who had again been sworn in as the prime minister of the recognized government just four months before Kabul fell to the Taliban. A 1999 Sandia National Laboratories report acknowledged Hekmatyar was bin Laden's closest Afghan ally (Richter 1999).
6. Even in 1997 the origins of the Taliban were murky to many Afghans and they were alternatively thought of as tools of the Pakistanis, the Saudis, or the Americans.

7. Redactions in the document indicate that there may have been another Taliban official present.

8. In fact, the Taliban shot down two Russian crews during its tenure. One escaped and the other was ransomed back to Russia at a cost of $1 million per soldier.

9. In 2010, Stanakzai was one of the original Taliban "diplomats"in Doha, Qatar, where he remained for many years (Nordland 2013, pars. 1, 12).

10. Rubin (1998, par. 25) argued that the Taliban represent an "ideological radicalization" of elements of the tribal code and that they do not strictly adhere to the tribal code.

11. The original draft of this resolution made no mention of terrorism. But in a revision entered on 8 May 1997 a paragraph was added that, "urges the Taliban and all parties in Afghanistan to cease providing safe haven to suspected terrorists or permitting Afghani [sic] territory to be used for terrorist training."

12. This Ehsanullah Ehsan should not be confused with the Pakistani Taliban spokesman of the same name.

REFERENCES

Albright, Madeline. 1996. Global Role of the US [Speech to Women's Foreign Policy Group]. C-Span, November 19. Video.

Albright, Madeline. 2005. *Madame Secretary: A Memoir*. New York: Miramax.

Asia: Those Not Very Nice People in Afghanistan. 1998. *The Economist*, 25 April 1998, 347(8065), 41.

Burleigh, Peter. 1998. The Situation in Afghanistan and Its Implications for International Peace and Security. 84th Plenary Meeting of the UN General Assembly, *Official Records*, 9 December 1998.

Burns, John F. 1997. In Afghanistan, a Triumph of Fundamentalism. *New York Times*, 26 May 1997. Web.

Burns, Nicholas. 1996. Daily Press Briefing [transcript]. 3 October 1996. Office of the Spokesman, US Department of State.

Christopher, Warren. 1996a. Dealing with the Taliban in Kabul [Secretary of State Christopher to US Embassy Islamabad]. 28 September 1996. US Department of State, document accessed at the National Security Archive, Washington, DC.

Christopher, Warren. 1996b. Afghanistan: Taliban Rep Won't Seek UN Seat For Now [Secretary of State Christopher to US Embassy Islamabad]. 11 December 1996. US Department of State, document accessed at the National Security Archive, Washington, DC.

Cochran, Charles L. 1968. De facto and de jure Recognition: Is There a Difference? *The American Journal of International Law* 62 (2): 457–460.

Coll, Steve. 2004. *Ghost Wars: The Secret History of the CIA, Afghanistan, and bin Laden, from the Soviet Invasion to September 10, 2001.* New York: Penguin Press.

Clinton, William J. 1998. Remarks on International Women's Day, 11 March 1998. *Weekly Compilation of Presidential Documents,* 16 March 1998, 34(11), 410–411.

Davies, Glyn. 1996a. Daily Press Briefing [transcript]. 28 September 1996. Office of the Spokesman, US Department of State, Washington, DC.

Davies, Glyn. 1996b. Daily Press Briefing [transcript]. September 1996. Office of the Spokesman, US Department of State, Washington, DC.

DCI Talking Points Regarding Operations Against Osama bin Laden. 1997. 25 August 1997. Central Intelligence Agency, document accessed at the National Security Archive, Washington, DC (The author of this document is the unnamed chief of the CIA's Counterterrorism Center).

Deutch, John M. 1996. Afghanistan: Taliban's Victory Impact. 30 September 1996. Central Intelligence Agency, document accessed at the National Security Archive, Washington, DC (This document was produced by the Office of the Director of Central Intelligence, but its exact author is unknown and is almost certainly not former Director of Central Intelligence John Deutch).

Dodd, Christopher. 1997. Senate Concurrent Resolution 6. 7 February 1997. 105th Congress, 1st Session. Government Publications Office.

Eastham, Alan. 1997. Afghanistan: The Taliban's Mullah Rabbani: Contender for Taliban Leadership? [from US Embassy Islamabad to Secretary of State Albright]. 7 April 1997. US Department of State, document accessed at the National Security Archive, Washington, DC.

Filkins, Dexter. 2001. The Legacy of the Taliban Is a Sad and Broken Land. *New York Times,* 31 December 2001. Web.

Filkins, Dexter. 2008. *The Forever War.* New York: Alfred A. Knopf.

Gannon, Kathy. 2005. *I Is for Infidel.* New York: Public Affairs.

Gnehm, Edward. 1997. The Situation in Afghanistan. 3765th Meeting of the United Nations Security Council. *Official Records of the Security Council,* 14 April 1997, pp. 19–20.

Gutman, Roy. 2008. *How We Missed the Story: Osama bin Laden, the Taliban, and the Hijacking of Afghanistan.* Washington, DC: United States Institute of Peace.

Hanson, Brad. 1997. Afghanistan: Taliban Agree to Visits of Militant Training Camps, Admit Bin Ladin Is Their Guest [from US Consulate Peshawar to Secretary of State Albright]. 9 January 1997. US Department of State, document accessed at the National Security Archive, Washington, DC.

IAC Intelligence Assessment. 1996. 17 October 1996. Privy Council Office's Intelligence Assessment Secretariat. Ottawa, Canada. Document accessed at the National Security Archive, Washington, DC.

Intelligence Report: Afghanistan: Taliban External Ambitions. 1998. 28 October 1998. US Department of State, document accessed at the National Security Archive, Washington, DC.

LeVine, Steve, and Raymond Bonner. 1998. Doubts Grow That Taliban Would Give up Terrorist Mastermind to the U.S. *New York Times*, 25 August 1998, p. A6.

Mackenzie, Richard. 1998. The United States and the Taliban. In *Fundamentalism Reborn? Afghanistan and the Taliban*, ed. William Maley, 90–103. New York: New York University Press.

Maloney, Carolyn. 1997. House Concurrent Resolution 156. 23 September 1997. 105th Congress, 1st Session. Government Publications Office.

Nordland, Rod. 2013. Peace Envoys from Taliban at Loose Ends in Qatar. *New York Times*, 9 April 2013. Web.

President Clinton: A Historic Commitment to International Human Rights. 1998. 11 March 1998. Office of the Press Secretary, The White House, accessed at US Department of State Archive. Web.

Rashid, Ahmed. 1998. Dropping in. *Far Eastern Economic Review*, 30 April 1998, 161(18), 29.

Rashid, Ahmed. 2009. *Descent into Chaos: The U.S. and the Disaster in Pakistan, Afghanistan, and Central Asia*. New York: Penguin.

Richter, Gary W. 1999. Osama bin Laden: A Case Study. 6 December 1999. Sandia National Laboratories, document accessed at the National Security Archive, Washington, DC.

Rubin, Barnett. 1998. Testimony on the Situation in Afghanistan before the United States Senate Committee on Foreign Relations. *Council on Foreign Relations*, 8 October 1998. Web.

Schulz, John J., and Linda Schulz. 1999. The Darkest of Ages: Afghan Women Under the Taliban. *Peace and Conflict: Journal of Peace Psychology* 5 (3): 237–254.

Simons, Thomas W. 1996a. Afghanistan: Taliban Official Says that Relations with Russia and Iran 'Tense' [from US Embassy Islamabad to Secretary of State Christopher]. 29 September 1996. US Department of State, document accessed at the National Security Archive, Washington, DC.

Simons, Thomas W. 1996b. Afghanistan: Taliban Seeks Low Profile Relations with the USG—At Least for Now [from US Embassy Islamabad to US Embassy Dhaka]. 8 October 1996. US Department of State, document accessed at the National Security Archive, Washington, DC.

Simons, Thomas W. 1996c. Afghanistan: Foreign Secretary Mulls Over Afghanistan [from US Embassy Islamabad to Secretary of State Christopher].

10 October 1996. US Department of State, document accessed at the National Security Archive, Washington, DC.

Simons, Thomas W. 1996d. Ambassador Meets Taliban: We Are the People [from US Embassy Islamabad to Secretary of State Christopher]. 12 November 1996. US Department of State, document accessed at the National Security Archive, Washington, DC.

Simons, Thomas W. 1996e. Afghanistan: Taliban Deny They Are Sheltering HUA Militants, Osama bin Laden [from US Embassy Islamabad to Secretary of State Christopher]. 12 November 1996. US Department of State, document accessed at the National Security Archive, Washington, DC.

Simons, Thomas W. 1997a. Afghani Taliban Shift Yar Mohammed from Herat to Ghazni [from US Embassy Islamabad to Secretary of State Christopher]. 2 January 1997. US Department of State, document accessed at the National Security Archive, Washington, DC.

Simons, Thomas W. 1997b. Scenesetter for Your Visit to Islamabad: Afghan Angle [from US Embassy Islamabad to Secretary of State Albright]. 16 January 1997. US Department of State, document accessed at the National Security Archive, Washington, DC.

Simons, Thomas W. 1997c. Pakistan Counterterrorism: Ambassador's Meeting with [redacted] February 6, on State Sponsor Designation [from US Embassy Islamabad to Secretary of State Albright]. 7 February 1997. US Department of State, document accessed at the National Security Archive, Washington, DC.

Simons, Thomas W. 1997d. Afghanistan: Raising Bin Ladin with the Taliban [from US Embassy Islamabad to Secretary of State Albright]. 4 March 1997. US Department of State, document accessed at the National Security Archive, Washington, DC.

Simons, Thomas W. 1997e. Official Informal—For SA Assistant Secretary Robin Raphel and SA/PAB (from US Embassy Islamabad to Secretary of State Albright). 10 March 1997. US Department of State, document accessed at the National Security Archive, Washington, DC.

Simons, Thomas W. 1997f. Afghanistan: Straight Talk with [redacted] [from US Embassy Islamabad to Secretary of State Albright]. 12 August 1997. US Department of State, document accessed at the National Security Archive, Washington, DC (The source is clearly a Pakistani government official).

Simons, Thomas W. 1997g. Afghanistan: [redacted] Briefs the Ambassador on His Activities. Pleads for Greater Activism By UN [from US Embassy Islamabad to Secretary of State Albright]. 27 August 1997. US Department of State, document accessed at the National Security Archive, Washington, DC (The source is clearly a Pakistani government official).

Simons, Thomas W. 1997h. Afghanistan: Taliban Decision-Making and Leadership Structure [from US Embassy Islamabad to Secretary of State

Albright]. 30 December 1997. US Department of State, document accessed at the National Security Archive, Washington, DC.

Simons, Thomas W. 1998a. Afghanistan: [redacted] Describes Pakistan's Current Thinking [from US Embassy Islamabad to Secretary of State Albright]. 9 March 1998. US Department of State, document accessed at the National Security Archive, Washington, DC.

Simons, Thomas W. 1998b. Bad News for Pak Afghan Policy: GOP Support for the Taliban Appears to Be Getting Stronger [from US Embassy Islamabad to Secretary of State Albright]. 1 July 1998. US Department of State, document accessed at the National Security Archive, Washington, DC.

Simons, Thomas W. 1998c. Afghanistan: In July 2 Meeting, [redacted] Defends Discriminatory Edicts on Women and Girls, and Controls on NGO's [from US Embassy Islamabad to Secretary of State Albright]. 2 July 1998. US Department of State, document accessed at the National Security Archive, Washington, DC.

Simons, Thomas W. 1998d. In Bilateral Focussed on Afghanistan, GOP Reviews Pak/Iran Effort; Inderfurth Expresses US Concerns About the Taliban [from US Embassy Islamabad to Secretary of State Albright]. 23 July 1998. US Department of State, document accessed at the National Security Archive, Washington, DC.

Talbott, Strobe. 1997. Afghanistan: Meeting with the Taliban [Secretary of State Albright to US Embassy Islamabad]. 11 December 1997. US Department of State, document accessed at the National Security Archive, Washington, DC.

Talking Points Regarding Osama bin Laden for DCI's 2 September 1998 SSCI Briefing. 2 September 1998. Central Intelligence Agency, document accessed at the National Security Archive, Washington, DC.

United Nations Security Council Resolution 1076 (22 October 1996). Web.

Wright, Lawrence. 2007. *The Looming Tower: Al-Qaeda and the Road to 9/11.* New York: Vintage.

CHAPTER 4

US/Taliban Relations and the Intervention of Domestic Politics

Abstract The Al Qaeda attacks in Kenya and Tanzania brought global attention to both Osama bin Laden and to the Taliban. President Clinton responded with cruise missile strikes against Al Qaeda training camps near Khost, Afghanistan. This chapter looks at US/Taliban relations in the year after that strike. This time period was categorized by extreme pressure on the Clinton Administration from American feminist groups not to recognize the Taliban as the legitimate government of Afghanistan. The Clinton Administration was publicly supportive of those groups but, in the field, the priority was Osama bin Laden. The US and the Taliban met repeatedly to find a compromise that would allow them to expel bin Laden. There were Taliban officials who disapproved of bin Laden's presence in Afghanistan, but domestic politics, and Mullah Omar's intransigence, made it difficult to work with Washington.

Keywords Afghanistan · Bill Clinton, Feminist Majority Foundation Mavis Leno · Taliban · Women's rights

The Al Qaeda attacks in Kenya and Tanzania brought global attention to both Osama bin Laden and to the Taliban. The Taliban's feelings about bin Laden or about the Africa attacks in particular were largely irrelevant; they were inextricably linked in the public imagination. Nevertheless, at the time, the Clinton Administration was clear to differentiate

© The Author(s) 2019
J. Cristol, *The United States and the Taliban before and after 9/11*,
https://doi.org/10.1007/978-3-319-97172-8_4

Al Qaeda from the Taliban in a way that the Bush Administration did not. President Bill Clinton (1998, p. 1460) remarked that Al Qaeda was "not sponsored by any state." This statement indicated that the Taliban would not be held responsible for Al Qaeda's actions.

President Clinton could not let the terrorist attacks go unpunished, but there was never any serious proposal to invade Afghanistan to go after Osama bin Laden. "It would not have been supported by the majority of our citizens or our allies, and would have been condemned throughout the Arab and Islamic Worlds," Secretary of State Madeline Albright (2005, p. 477) remarked. In his memoirs, President Clinton (2004, p. 804) wrote that, "It was clear to me that the senior military didn't want to [invade Afghanistan]."[1] President Clinton settled on cruise missile strikes against targets in Sudan and Afghanistan.

However, the target in Sudan, thought to be a site for Al Qaeda chemical weapons production, turned out to be a harmless pharmaceutical plant.[2] In Afghanistan, the US fired cruise missiles at terrorist training camps in Khost, missing bin Laden by just a few hours (National Commission on Terrorist Attacks Against the United States 2004, p. 117).[3] These missile strikes came, "just as the Taliban prepared to campaign for international diplomatic recognition" (Rubin 1998, par. 1). Perhaps counterintuitively, the missile strike inside Afghanistan caused the Taliban to focus even more attention on developing a good relationship with the United States. And President Clinton's care not to link the Taliban to Al Qaeda left the door open to working with the Taliban on this and other issues.

Before the 7 August 1998 embassy bombings, President Clinton had very little to say on the matter of the Taliban. Of course, it is neither possible to completely reconstruct every meeting in the White House during the Clinton Administration, nor can we know how much time he devoted to thinking about Afghanistan. However, it is quite clear from his daily schedules that the majority of his time spent on foreign policy concerned Northern Ireland, the Balkans, Haiti, and Israel. There was never a meeting solely devoted to Afghanistan, while there were many for each of the above regions. In fact, according to Ahmed Rashid (2010, p. 178), "Secretary of State Warren Christopher never publicly mentioned Afghanistan once during his entire tenure."

President Clinton was under tremendous pressure from his own family, his own political staff, and the feminist lobby not to recognize the Taliban government. Barnett Rubin, perhaps America's top expert on

Afghanistan, testified before the Senate Foreign Relations Committee that, "The organization of an influential lobbying network of feminist, human rights, and humanitarian groups, supported by some Afghan women exiles in the United States... have made gender policies into a political issue. These networks include key constituencies of President Clinton and the Democratic Party" (1998, par. 73). This pressure was difficult for Clinton to resist. And while this pressure was effective for years, it worked only so long as Clinton saw nothing to be gained from recognizing the Taliban government; and between 1998 and 2001, there was a gradual shift in priorities. The Taliban's treatment of women and girls took a backseat to the sanctuary they provided for Osama bin Laden and his Al Qaeda network. Outwardly, the administration was focused on women's rights, but, behind-the-scenes, there was the potential for compromise. It was the Taliban who would prove uncompromising.

In the feminist journal *Off Our Backs*, Carol Ann Douglas (1998, p. 5) writes, "Feminist groups... mobilized to pressure the Clinton administration not to recognize the Taliban fundamentalist self-proclaimed government in Afghanistan." And there was no group that focused on this issue more singularly than the Feminist Majority Foundation, which aggressively lobbied the Clinton Administration not to recognize the Taliban. The public face of the Feminist Majority's campaign against the Taliban was Mavis Leno. Ms. Leno joined the Feminist Majority Foundation in 1996 after meeting Peg Yorkin, the Foundation's chair, at a *New Yorker* luncheon celebrating the magazine's all-female issue (Hoban 2000, par. 5). Mavis Leno became the chair of the Feminist Majority's "Campaign to Stop Gender Apartheid in Afghanistan." She and her husband, *The Tonight Show* host Jay Leno, donated $100,000 to the campaign, and Ms. Leno said she, "will never, ever abandon these women" (Chang 1999, par. 2). The Feminist Majority sent the White House and State Department "100,000 petitions, letters, e-mails, and faxes" (Chang 1999, par. 3). They called for aid to be withheld from countries that recognize the Taliban, assistance for Afghan women in Afghanistan, and an increase in US admission of female Afghan refugees. Three hundred groups joined the Feminist Majority's campaign (Rashid 2010, p. 182).

The State Department took a mixed view of Leno's efforts. The Feminist Majority succeeded in "winning" 17 visas for Afghan women, about which one State Department official said, "For the Feminist Majority to push individual cases that come to Mavis Leno's attention through a friend who knows an Afghan woman who has access to a fax machine is just not fair or appropriate" (Chang 1999, par. 6). She was also criticized by a "tiny but noisy pro-Taliban lobby" including Laili Helms, daughter-in-law of former CIA chief Richard Helms, "who is convinced the Taliban is good for Afghanistan and that life is better now that someone is in charge after years of civil war" (Carlson 1999, par. 3). *Off Our Backs* published a spread titled, "Afghanistan: The Biggest Prison for Women in the World." It acknowledged that women under the Taliban gained security from such atrocities as "parts of their body... removed one by one as the women still lived," but "at the price of being confined to their homes" (Afghan Women's Network 1997, p. 13). Ms. Leno saw no grey areas and was undeterred by any such criticism.

Ms. Leno had never been a public figure, but she began to make a series of high profile appearances advocating for Afghan women. She appeared on *The Tonight Show* for the first time ever in March 1999. And she argued in *US Weekly* that Afghan women had had equal rights since the 1960s, but "overnight when the Taliban came in, they were stripped of every right a human being can have" (Hoban 2000, par. 4).[4] Ms. Leno's work was greeted with rapture—*Time Magazine* even wrote that "Leno and the Feminist Majority look like the best chance for [Afghan refugees] to go home again" (Carlson 1999, par. 5). Ms. Leno (1999, par. 2) wrote to "Dear Abby," "Reporters told me the Afghan situation had received so little coverage because their editors thought Americans aren't interested in this kind of news." She argued that the Taliban were responding to the Feminist Majority's pressure campaign by easing some restrictions including allowing some home-schooling for girls and single-sex hospital wards for women (Leno 1999, par. 5). And while it is unclear if they had any real impact on the Taliban, they did attract the attention of the administration and focused its attention on the non-recognition of the Taliban government.

First Lady Hilary Clinton had long been focused on women's issues, including the plight of women under the Taliban. On International Women's Day in 1997, Mrs. Clinton (2003, p. 393), "spoke out strongly against the barbaric rule of the Taliban in Afghanistan." At a White House event for Human Rights Day, she spoke at length about the Taliban and the rights of women. She said (1998, pars. 14, 19) that, "Perhaps the most egregious and systematic trampling of fundamental human rights of any person is taking place in Afghanistan today against women.... We cannot allow these terrible crimes against women and girls.... to continue with impunity.... We must do everything in our power to stop it."

Clinton wrote in her 2003 memoir *Living History*, "I believed that the United States should not recognize their government because of its oppression of women; nor should American business enter into contacts for pipeline construction or any other commercial enterprise" (p. 393).

President Clinton publicly acknowledged the work of the Feminist Majority Foundation in the East Room of the White House at the Sixth Millennium Evening on 15 March 1999. The "Millennium Evenings" were a series of lectures and performances held in the White House and broadcast to the American people. The theme of the Sixth Millennium Evening was "Women as Citizen: Vital Voices Through the Century." Clinton (1999a, p. 383) called attention to the plight of Afghan women and said, "I'm going to have a meeting with some of [the Feminist Majority Foundation's] leaders pretty soon to talk about what more I can do, aside *from not recognizing the Taliban* and speaking against it [emphasis added]." Clinton talked about the need for people to support the Feminist Majority and to highlight what is happening in Afghanistan. The president later met with members of the Feminist Majority Foundation and "talked about... what other things we could do to put pressure on the Taliban" (Clinton 1999d, p. 558).

In that meeting, the group asked Clinton to declare the Taliban a "Foreign Terrorist Organization." Mavis Leno said that they, "asked him to tell us that the United States under his administration would never recognize the Taliban" (Gutman 2008, p. 175). He promised not to unless they "improve their human rights record on women's issues" (Gutman 2008, p. 176). The Feminist Majority Foundation was asking for extreme measures. The Taliban had not undertaken any terrorist acts themselves, and non-recognition was not necessarily the answer to the plight of Afghanistan's women.

Secretary Albright also voiced her disapproval of the Taliban's treatment of women. She said (2005, p. 462) to a local reporter in Pakistan that, "We are opposed to the Taliban because of... their despicable treatment of women and children and their general lack of respect for human dignity." After meeting with female Afghan ex-patriots, she "told them that I would never forget my visit with them and that America would do everything it could to help" (Albright 2005, p. 462). Mullah Mohammed Omar responded to Albright's statement. On the state-run Radio Shariat, he said that she had "an incorrect knowledge of reality"

(Maley 2000, fn. 75). He explained that the only human rights allowed by the Taliban come from the Koran. He made clear his opinion about women's rights and women's education: "Let us state what sort of education the United Nations wants—This is a big infidel policy which gives such obscene freedom to women" (Mantilla 1998, p. 3). He explained that increased rights for women would lead to adultery, which in turn would bring about the "destruction of Islam" (Mantilla 1998, p. 3). He also said, "In any Islamic country where adultery becomes common, that country is destroyed and enters the domination of the infidels because their men become like women and women cannot defend themselves" (Mantilla 1998, p. 3). This was his only response to international criticism of any kind and showed just how provincial Omar's views of women were.

The fact that the State Department was actively negotiating with the Taliban on a variety of issues does not mean that Clinton and Albright's remarks were insincere. They were sincere in their desire not to recognize the Taliban because they miscalculated the importance of Afghanistan to American national interests. If events in Afghanistan could not impact the United States, it would be entirely proper to isolate the Taliban based on their treatment of women and girls. But the Al Qaeda embassy attacks showed that what happened in Afghanistan could impact America, and Washington would have no choice but to continue to work with the Taliban. And despite Rubin's (1998, par. 3) testimony that no "dialogue is possible for some time," the dialogue did indeed continue.

Though President Clinton seemed to make it quite clear that he would not accept a Taliban government in Afghanistan, Columbia University's Steve Coll writes in *Ghost Wars* (2004, p. 129) that, at first, "The Americans accepted [the Taliban's] legitimacy." The State Department's position on the Taliban changed as a result of the embassy bombings. It became more circumspect in its dealings with the Taliban, and was unsure of the Taliban's sincerity in its negotiations, but it still made every effort to secure bin Laden from the Taliban, potentially even at the expense of Afghan women's rights. In a meeting between US Ambassador to Pakistan William Milam and Pakistani Foreign Minister Shamshad Ahmed, Milan told Ahmed that while the US could discuss the "status of women and girls" with the Taliban, there was no flexibility when it came to Osama bin Laden. It was of "paramount interest... [to] secure the immediate extradition of bin Laden from the country"

(Milam 1998c). And while some Taliban officials were willing to part with bin Laden and build a better relationship with the United States, the Taliban's leader had some thoughts to share on the matter.

Mullah Omar's reaction to the 20 August missile strike was heated. He did not seem to hear President Clinton's message. "It is not only an attack against Osama bin Laden, but also an attack against the entire people of Afghanistan," said Omar, who also called the reprisal a "brazen manifestation of enmity against the Afghan nation" (Simons 1998a). Omar's position on bin Laden was clear, "We will never hand over bin Laden to anyone and (will) protect him with our blood at all cost" (Simons 1998a). This fiery rhetoric was designed for public consumption. Behind closed doors, he was more circumspect, though still unwilling to hand over bin Laden. The people's reaction to the Khost missile strikes was more muted than some Americans anticipated. The abandoned US embassy was overrun, but there were no injuries and no mass riots in Afghanistan's cities.

Mullah Omar's public statements were not surprising. What *were* genuinely shocking were the events of 22 August. Pakistan/Afghanistan/Bangladesh (PAB) Office Director Michael Malinowski was on a scheduled phone call with low-level Taliban officials when one of them asked him if he was willing to speak to a top leader. The top leader was Mullah Omar himself. This contact was the only instance of a real time conversation between Omar and an American official.[5] Secretary Albright (2005, p. 469) said that the call was "unprecedented. Omar almost never spoke to Westerners."

Malinowski said to Omar that there was a lot to talk about, especially Osama bin Laden. Omar replied that he was open to talking, but had no particular message to convey. Omar showed his awareness of American politics and said that Clinton should be forced to resign, "to rebuild US popularity in the Islamic world and because of his current domestic political difficulties," referring to the Monica Lewinsky scandal. Omar repeated a classic Taliban talking-point that there was no evidence that bin Laden had been involved in terrorism while in Afghanistan. He warned Malinowski that the missile strikes would be counterproductive and would increase solidarity against the US (Albright 1998b).

Malinowski responded by highlighting that there was considerable evidence against Osama bin Laden, and that the US acted in self-defense against Al Qaeda. The strikes were not directed against the Afghan people or against the Taliban. Malinowski also pointed out that bin Laden himself had violated the tradition of Pashtunwali: "bin Laden [is] like a guest who was shouting at his neighbors out of the host's window." Omar believed that, "Getting rid of one individual would not end the problems posed to the US by the Islamic world" (Albright 1998b). Despite his best efforts to persuade Omar that the Taliban's best interests would be served by expelling bin Laden, Omar did not give in.

Malinowski observed that Omar was "careful and controlled," cordial and attentive, and did not bluster or make threats. He said that the contact was remarkable and that the Taliban were serious about dialogue—Omar even said he was open to a direct and secure line of communication—but that, "Doesn't mean they'll do the right thing." Malinowski remarked that Omar "emphasized that this was his best advice" and that his tone was "in no way threatening" (Albright 1998b).

The day after the phone call Secretary Albright sent instructions to the US embassy in Islamabad and to the consulate in Peshawar. The diplomats were tasked to probe the seriousness of the Taliban's readiness to discuss Osama bin Laden, "with the realization that it could turn out to be a ploy for recognition or other benefits." The points to be conveyed were that the US was interested in a "serious dialogue" using Islamabad as a secret channel. They should reiterate that the attack on Khost was against bin Laden, not against the Taliban and that the US, "in no way wanted to... damage the Taliban." After years of dealing with the Taliban, it was clear to the US that they would respond by claiming to need evidence that bin Laden was behind the attacks. In response, the Americans were to say that the Taliban has evidence and that the US knows that the Taliban knows, "What [he] says, what he does, and who he meets" (Albright 1998a). The US was very clear that they wanted the Taliban to expel bin Laden immediately.

Mullah Omar was unwilling to turn bin Laden over to the Americans, but that did not mean he was happy with the lanky Saudi terrorist. The Pakistani newspaper *The News* reported that Omar, referring to the Taliban and Al Qaeda, said, "There cannot be two different and parallel emirates in Afghanistan. We have a central Taliban-led authority ruling the country and it ought to be obeyed" (Simons 1998b). Omar reportedly sent an emissary to bin Laden to tell him to let Afghanistan, rather than Al Qaeda, respond to the US. Omar was upset that bin Laden called for retaliation against America, which the Taliban still hoped would be a friend. A still-classified source told the US embassy that, "Omar is coming under increasing pressure from other Taliban leaders concerning the presence of bin Laden in Afghanistan" (Simons 1998b). Tayyib Husseini at the Taliban embassy in Pakistan said that the Taliban should not protect bin Laden "when it is clearly antagonizing the US and other countries" (Simons 1998b). Kandahar governor Mullah Hassan was said to be taking the lead on pressuring Omar, and an inner shura meeting regarding bin Laden was held on 22–23 August (Simons 1998b). Some prominent members of the Taliban were lukewarm about bin Laden's presence, but others rallied behind him. Two Taliban religious leaders issued a fatwa requiring Muslims to protect bin Laden (Eastham 1998a).

In September, the US acknowledged that, "The Taliban leadership appears to be split" about Osama bin Laden's presence in Afghanistan. The same cable indicates that a reliable, redacted source said that Taliban deputy head Mohammed Rabbani led an anti-bin Laden camp within the Taliban (Talbott 1998a). Deputy Foreign Minister Abdul Jalil referred to bin Laden as "an enemy" (Milam 1998d). Even Taliban Intelligence Chief Mullah Mohammed Khaksar was opposed to bin Laden's presence (Gannon 2005, p. 25). Both sides agreed, however, that if he stayed, his "political activities" would have to be strictly controlled (Talbott 1998a).

The Americans were not the only ones who wanted bin Laden; on 19 September, Saudi Intelligence Chief Turki al-Faisel met with Mullah Omar and asked him for bin Laden. Omar replied by criticizing Saudi Arabia for allowing American troops on its territory.[6] In response, Riyadh downgraded its ties with the Taliban (Milam 1998b). Days later, Saudi Arabia stopped issuing visas, including Hajj visas, for the Taliban (Eastham 1998d). Bin Laden gave a series of interviews to Pakistani newspapers, where he praised the Taliban, saying that they were "like the state of Medina in the early days of Islam" (Eastham 1998e).

The United States and the Taliban held two meetings about bin Laden on 13 September. Deputy Chief of Mission in Islamabad Alan Eastham met with Maulawi Wakil Ahmed and later met with Abdul Hakim Mujahid, who had been appointed to head the Taliban's relations with the United States. Ahmed told Eastham that the Taliban had taken away bin Laden's "instruments of communication." Mujahid claimed that 80% of the Taliban leadership opposed bin Laden's presence, but Mullah Omar "is the major supporter of bin Laden" and thus it was a difficult matter to discuss within Taliban circles. Nobody wanted to oppose Mullah Omar. Mujahid confirmed that Rabbani opposed bin Laden's presence. He asked that the US be patient because the Taliban could not expel bin Laden because of pressure from other Muslims, but that after the war he would be dealt with. Ahmed admitted that the Taliban's foreign policy "was a disaster." The Taliban were "not used to governing" and it would take a long time to become a normal government. Nevertheless, he believed that the US and Taliban would "inevitably [be] drawn together because of regional factors including a common dislike of Iran." On the issue of women's rights, Ahmed said that after the war was over, women's rights would be dealt with, and he provided several citations from the Koran and the Sunna that supported equal rights for women (Milam 1998a).

Eastham inquired about the preservation of two giant statues of the Buddha in Bamiyan. Ahmed said that Omar had ordered the statues protected (Milam 1998a). The statues were ultimately destroyed. Pakistan sent representatives to Kandahar to persuade Omar not to destroy the statues, but Al Qaeda had already persuaded him to destroy them. Ambassador Milam said that, "The Taliban had become so dependent on Al Qaeda that they didn't really need the Pakistanis any more" (Filkins 2001, par. 64). Taliban Envoy Sayed Rahmatullah Hashemi said that a council of religious scholars ordered the destruction in a fit of pique over funds being made available to save the statues, but not for "children dying of malnutrition" (Crossette 2001, p. A9).

Days after Ahmed reported that Rabbani opposed bin Laden's presence, 1500 ulema met in Kabul to discuss five questions—four about the possibility of war with Iran. Also on the agenda was a debate about the merits of Omar vs. Rabbani's view of Osama bin Laden (Talbott 1998a). The US embassy in Islamabad saw unconfirmed reports of a 25 September coup led by Rabbani that resulted in 50 military officials arrested (Milam 1998b). Coll (2004, p. 514) reports that, by 1999, "Mullah Omar had reportedly executed Taliban dissenters over [the bin Laden] issue." Rabbani was not one of them and there is no definitive evidence that he was involved in any coup attempt. Rabbani died of cancer at a hospital in Islamabad on 16 April 2001 (Dugger 2001, par. 1).

Mullah Omar sent an unexpected fax from Kandahar to the State Department on 24 September 1998. He took a more aggressive tone in the fax than he did in his phone call with Malinowski.[7] The fax was addressed to "The Leadership of the United States Government" and contained Omar's "Good Advice for Selecting a Policy Appropriate to Your Elevated Status." The short message informed the Americans that the Taliban's platform "offers no harm to the US." He acknowledged

America's help fighting the Russians but pointed out that it was the Afghan people that sacrificed. The Taliban policy "is real Islamic policy. We cannot change it.... Almighty God has obligated us to follow this policy" (Albright 1998c). He ended by pointing out that Americans are Christians and Christians help Muslims.

One week later, the US was ready with a response to be given to both Mullah Omar and Mullah Rabbani. The US gave its usual talking points. It was ready to have a serious and confidential dialogue with the Taliban. It had long feelings of friendship with, and respect for, the Afghan people. The response pointed out that the US funded many projects in Afghanistan and was interested in helping to repair the country, and that the US was not anti-Islam: "Americans respect and honor Islam." Conversely, Osama bin Laden kills Muslims and threatens Americans. Anticipating the Taliban's reversion to the Pashtunwali argument, "Those who abuse your hospitality... no longer deserve to be received and treated as friends." The US wanted friendship with the Taliban, but made it clear that the Taliban would be held responsible for further acts by the "Osama bin Laden network" so long as they provided him sanctuary (Albright 1998c).

Over the following months, various schemes and proposals to reach an agreeable compromise on bin Laden were discussed. One Pakistani official suggested to the Americans that the Taliban wanted to get rid of bin Laden and listed three possibilities: (1) he could be judged by Saudi and Afghan clerics (a delegation could visit Riyadh to work out the details);[8] (2) the Taliban could sell bin Laden to the United States; or (3) the Taliban would judge him themselves based on the 1996 Khobar Towers bombing in Saudi Arabia, which killed 20 people. He would be summarily executed if found guilty, but only if there were Muslim victims. He reported that many still-classified Taliban concluded that bin Laden was more trouble than he was worth and that they could extract something from the US for him (Milam 1998d). How they expected to handle Mullah Omar was not clear.

The Taliban requested a meeting in Kandahar to discuss the matter further, but it was deemed too unsafe for Americans and other venues were suggested. Though much of the information remains classified it appears as though the United States was willing to pay almost any price for bin Laden, and would almost certainly have recognized the Taliban, and offered millions of dollars in cash plus millions in humanitarian aid for him (Milam 1998d). Coll (2004, p. 431) writes that, "The underlying premise of this outreach, rarely stated aloud… was to trade US diplomatic recognition of the Taliban as Afghanistan's legitimate government in exchange for custody of Osama bin Laden." Pressure to moderate their position on women's rights could be applied once bin Laden was out of Afghanistan.

On 12 October, Ambassador Milam and a staffer met with Wakil Ahmed and Sayed Rahman Haqqani,[9] the new Taliban chargé d'affaires in Islamabad. Milam mentioned women and girls, but said that, "The primary issue for the US is terrorism." Ahmed said that when the Taliban first took over, they asked Saudi Arabia if they wanted bin Laden, but the Saudis said to keep him. Now, "The Taliban [take] seriously Saudi and US demands to expel bin Laden." Despite the seriousness of the situation, Ahmed pushed back harder than usual. Not only did he say that the Taliban would be overthrown if they gave up bin Laden, and that they did not believe he was responsible for the embassy attacks, but he also repeated Omar's position that the US should leave Saudi Arabia. Ahmed emphasized the need for a sharia trial. The tone was cordial, but serious, and Milam remarked that a solution to the bin Laden situation "may be a mite more possible now" (Milam 1998e). The idea that it was politically difficult for the Taliban to turn over bin Laden is well-expressed in a Sandia Labs report that pointed out that it was as politically difficult for conservatives in Afghanistan to give bin Laden to the US as it would be for the US to give Oliver North to Vietnam (Richter 1999).

The question of recognizing the Taliban government was never far from the surface. In a memorandum for Secretary Albright, Milam (1998f) suggested that if the Taliban expel bin Laden, there could "possibly even [be] some flexibility on the UN seat." If they do not, he suggested that Saudi Arabia and the US should "work against them in every way to ensure they never obtain 'recognition' or international reconstruction assistance" (Milam 1998f). Unfortunately, "[There is] little indication that anything we have said on bin Laden to the Taliban has registered with Mullah Omar" Milam (1998f) added. It is possible, however, that everything the US said about bin Laden had registered, but that Omar genuinely believed that he received divine guidance.

If you think it is frustrating to read about how many times the US pressed the bin Laden issue with the Taliban, imagine actually being a Talib. They became more obstinate as time went on, and gave the US until 20 November to provide them with evidence against bin Laden. "If by then there is nothing, we will close the case and in our eyes he will be acquitted," said Taliban Spokesman Abdul Hai Mutmain (Milam 1998g). It did not help Washington's cause that Saudi Minister of the Interior Prince Nayef bin Abdulaziz publicly absolved bin Laden of the Khobar Towers bombing (Milam 1998g).

Things did not improve when Milam met with Haqqani again on 11 November. At this point, the Taliban insisted that bin Laden was both totally under control and that he must be tried by the Taliban (as opposed to Saudi Arabia). Milam provided him with a copy of the 6 November US District Court of Southern New York indictment of bin Laden for "conspiracy to attack US facilities overseas and to kill American citizens," as well as transcripts of bin Laden's May 1997 CNN interview and June 1998 ABC interview. Haqqani said that bin Laden cannot be held accountable for all of his past followers. In a marked change in approach, Haqqani implied that US citizens would not be safe if bin Laden were apprehended. This vague threat did not seem to be of particular cause for concern, because, while Haqqani was a reliable conduit to Omar, he was "not particularly high-ranking." Milam informed Haqqani that the US knew bin Laden was plotting something against the United States, and that Washington would hold the Taliban responsible for it (Talbott 1998b).

On 28 November, in a conversation between Wakil Ahmed and Eastham, Ahmed provided an additional incentive for the US to recognize the Taliban government—if recognized and given compensation for farmers, the Taliban would "ban the growth of poppies." Ahmed also said that the Taliban did not oppose *educating* women, only co-ed education. Unfortunately, he repeated the "no evidence" bin Laden talking point. Eastham told him that the US could not promise not to strike the Taliban if the bin Laden "problem was not resolved." The potential for directly attacking the Taliban was now being openly discussed. Ahmed said he hoped bin Laden would just leave on his own. In a new and interesting twist, Ahmed said that, "Saddam Hussein was the root cause of all of these problems." In a dig at his Taliban guest, Eastham said that the Taliban was not behaving like a government if it was so scared it would fall if it turned over bin Laden (Eastham 1998b). The two men met again two weeks later and had the same conversation. It was as if they were talking into thin air.

The US continued to press the Taliban across all fronts. In New York, Ambassador Nancy Soderberg spoke to the UN Security Council on 8 December 1998 in support of UNSCR 1214: "We call on all Afghan factions, particularly the Taliban, to abide by this and earlier resolutions and ensure that all indicted terrorists on their soil are brought to justice." She said that, "Afghanistan-based terrorism has become a plague." The resolution demanded that: the Taliban investigate the deaths of UN workers in Kabul and Jalalabad; there be an investigation into the deaths of the Iranian diplomats in Mazar-i-Sharif; "the Afghan factions put an end to discrimination against girls and women"; and that "the Taliban stop providing sanctuary and training for international terrorists and their organizations." "The Taliban in particular must respect the rights of the Afghan people, especially women and girls, as well as minorities," said Ambassador Soderberg (1998, p. 7). The next day, US UN chargé d'affaires Peter Burleigh (1998) addressed the General Assembly and called for, "the expulsion of terrorists such as Osama bin Laden."

The Taliban said repeatedly that bin Laden was prohibited from speaking to the press, but a series of high profile interviews showed that the Taliban was either unable or unwilling to control bin Laden. They were, however, astute enough to realize that Washington would be upset. On 30 December, Eastham met with a "downcast" Haqqani. Eastham slammed the Taliban based on the previous Taliban assurances that bin Laden could not speak to the press. Haqqani said that bin Laden had repeatedly asked the Taliban for permission to give interviews, but they had always denied permission. This time they agreed, so that he could deny his involvement in terrorism and renounce terrorism—bin Laden had hoodwinked them! Haqqani reiterated that bin Laden's policy was not the Taliban's policy and that he would not be permitted to give any additional interviews. Eastham recalled that it was "culturally important for Afghans to be seen as honoring their word" and it was "obviously difficult for Haqqani to admit that the Taliban had not been able to do this." Nevertheless, "A simpleton could have seen the danger of putting him in front of the press" (Eastham 1998f).

The Taliban government's situation did not improve in 1999. It seemed as if its winning streak may have ended. They were running low on money, Pakistan was having economic problems, and Saudi Arabia had cut off aid. In addition, their supply lines were overstretched. Their primary source of funding was from wealthy Emiratis and Qataris (Milam 1999a). And the $11.7 million that Afghanistan earned from overflight rights for civilian airliners was held at a bank in Switzerland, which the Taliban government could not access because it was unrecognized ("Ariana Afghan Airlines: Assets" 1999). And while bin Laden did give the Taliban financial support, according to the State Department, it was "probably not enough to make a significant difference in their cash balance" (Milam 1999a). The poor financial situation left an opening for further dependence on bin Laden.

The meetings between the Taliban and the United States increased in both frequency and rank, but still followed the same script. Assistant Secretary of State for South Asia Karl Inderfurth and State Department Coordinator for Counterterrorism Michael Sheehan met with Jalil at the US ambassador's residence in Islamabad. Jalil acknowledged that bin Laden was "increasingly a burden on Afghanistan," but that Pashtunwali did not allow them to force his exit. Jalil said there was no way he could be operating a terrorist network and asked for evidence against bin Laden, but the evidence that Sheehan provided was unconvincing, as any evidence provided likely would have been (Inderfurth 2001, p. M3). The Taliban were unwilling to acknowledge Osama bin Laden's responsibility for acts that bin Laden himself had expressed pride in carrying out.

The Taliban's continued intransigence, combined with the growing threat from bin Laden, led to a rethink about the possibility of good relations with the Taliban. Inderfurth wrote to Secretary Albright that, "We may have to consider the Taliban to be an intrinsic enemy of the US and a new international pariah state." However, this was not ideal, and he said that, "We are not there yet and we do not want to be there." Nevertheless, the Taliban were not making it easy to work with them: "[Its] policies now preclude us... from offering the Taliban what it wants—recognition as the rulers of Afghanistan." This would be possible "if and only if" the Taliban not only turned over bin Laden, but also dealt with opium crops and rectified their "treatment of women and girls" (Inderfurth 1999). The question of the treatment of women by the Taliban may have been sublimated in the push to acquire Osama bin Laden, but it was not forgotten in Washington and, increasingly, in Los Angeles.

California senator Barbara Boxer introduced a Senate Resolution "expressing the sense of the Senate regarding the treatment of women and girls by the Taliban in Afghanistan" (1999).[10] The text was largely the same as previous resolutions and maintained the provision that the president should do everything possible to prevent the Taliban from gaining the UN seat, and that he should not recognize the Taliban government unless it took the actions to improve the situation of women that were listed in previous resolutions (Boxer 1999). The *Far Eastern*

Economic Review reported that the Taliban's chances at recognition from the US or UN was "practically nonexistent," and quoted Barnett Rubin saying, "Right now the chances of diplomatic recognition are nil" (Dhume 1999, p. 23). There was little chance that the US could recognize the Taliban so long as it both continued to provide a safe haven for Osama bin Laden and it continued to oppress women. It was the latter issue that had continued resonance in US domestic politics. The Clinton Administration continued to publicly voice solidarity with Afghanistan's women.

On the South Lawn Pavillon of the White House, President Clinton said of Afghanistan's women, "America cares about those women. America cares about the little girls. America cares about the male sons of the widows who have been plundered there. That's what your country stands for" (Clinton 1999b, p. 487). Just a few weeks later, in the "question and answer" period of a discussion titled "The Perils of Indifference: Lessons Learned from a Violent Century" held as part of the White House's Seventh Millennium Evening, an internet-questioner asked, "Are human rights different in various locales?" In response, Clinton (1999c, p. 635) said that they are different in different countries, but not, "because people can use their own cultures or religion as an excuse to repress women and young girls, for example, the way the Taliban does in Afghanistan," it's because countries can do more than the minimum if they so choose. He also voiced his approval for the "vocal opposition [to the Taliban] among members of the Muslim community around the world who feel that they can say this and not be betraying their faith" (Clinton 1999c, p. 636).

Just a few days later in the Grand Ballroom of the Fairmont Hotel in San Francisco, Clinton held another "question and answer" session, this time with the American Society of Newspaper Editors. One questioner listed at length some examples of the Taliban's treatment of women and pointed out that the US had supported the *mujahedeen*, some of whom became Taliban or Taliban-affiliated. Clinton was asked if the US has an "obligation to [the] 11.5 million women and girls, because of our... former relationship [to the Taliban]?" Clinton replied, "I absolutely do." He went on to say that, "I think that what has happened to the women and children of Afghanistan is atrocious.... I think it is one of the worst examples of systematic human rights abuses in the world today, and a terrible perversion of Islam" (Clinton 1999d, p. 651). He referred to his meeting with the Feminist Majority, which had not relented in its campaign against the Taliban.

Jay and Mavis Leno held a Hollywood fundraiser on 29 March 1999 at the Directors Guild of America Theatre.[11] Lionel Ritchie performed and Sidney Poitier spoke to the crowd (Carlson 1999, par. 2). The foundation lobbied for the US to admit more refugees and attempted to set up scholarships for Afghan women to attend college in the United States (Mann 1999, p. C11). 130 feminist and human rights groups joined with the FMF to draw attention to the Taliban's human rights abuses (Dhume 1999, p. 23).

Congress was fully on board with the Feminist Majority Foundation's campaign against normalization of the Taliban. The House of Representatives expressed its sentiment that, "The United States should seek to prevent any Taliban-led government in Afghanistan from obtaining a seat in the United Nations, and should refuse to recognize any Afghan government, while gross violation of human rights persist against women and girls there" (Maloney and Rohrbacher 1999). The House Resolution was introduced by Carolyn Maloney and California congressman Dana Rohrbacher. After detailing the deprivations that women under the Taliban faced, it effectively called on the Taliban to allow women to participate in "civil, economic, and social life" along with the reopening of schools, freedom of movement, and equal access to health facilities and humanitarian aid (Maloney and Rohrbacher 1999).

But the American diplomats in Pakistan were singularly focused on Osama bin Laden. The Taliban, for their part, were grasping at straws. In a meeting with Ambassador Milam, Haqqani told him that bin Laden had left their territory and let him know that someone might attack the US and make it look like the Taliban did it. He also gave Milam the impression that the "Taliban have been working quietly to urge bin Laden to leave the country voluntarily" (Milam 1999b). The CIA had reached the same assessment, reporting that, "Some Taliban [were] reportedly contemplating how to effect his departure" ("DCI UBL Update" 1999). However, none of these efforts would matter because, the CIA correctly concluded, Mullah Omar would never agree to turn over bin Laden ("DCI UBL Update" 1999).

President Clinton signed an executive order "imposing financial and other commercial sanctions on the Afghan Taliban for its support of Osama bin Laden and his terrorist network." In his statement accompanying the signing of the order he said that, "The United States has tried repeatedly, directly and working with other governments, to persuade the Taliban to expel bin Laden to the United States for trial or, if that is not possible, to a third country where he will face justice for his crimes, and to end the safe haven it gives to bin Laden's network..... These efforts have failed." He said that, "It is not aimed at the people of Afghanistan, but at the Taliban" (Clinton 1999f, p. 1285). In a major shift in policy, the US actions were now aimed not just at Al Qaeda, but also the Taliban.

In President Clinton's letter to congressional leaders explaining his action, he reported that, "The actions and policies of the Afghan Taliban pose an unusual and extraordinary threat to the national security and foreign policy of the United States" because of its safe haven for Osama bin Laden and Al Qaeda. The order prohibited Americans from dealing with the Taliban, prohibited the export or import of "goods, software, technology (including technical data), or services" to or from the territory held by the Taliban or to or from the Taliban itself. Clinton (1999e, p. 1283) said that, "The measures taken in this order will immediately demonstrate to the Taliban the seriousness of our concern over its support for terrorists and terrorist networks, and increase the isolation of the Taliban.... It is particularly important for the United States to demonstrate to the Taliban the necessity of conforming to accepted norms of international behavior." In response to Clinton's executive order, Taliban Information Minister Mullah Amir Khan Mottaqi said, "Clinton is just hounding bin Laden and the Taliban to cover up his own inadequacies and failings" (Rashid 1999b, p. 9).

The United States was correct in its assessment that prominent Taliban leaders were opposed to Osama bin Laden's presence in Afghanistan. It was perhaps not unreasonable to continue these discussions. But one year after the Al Qaeda embassy attacks, the situation had only gotten worse. Mullah Omar had consolidated his power and "may have become more sympathetic to pan-Islamist thinking" (Eastham 1998g). Rabbani's influence declined. And bin Laden was not abiding by his agreement with the Taliban to refrain from "political" activity. He planned an attack on the US embassy in Albania, but the plot was foiled ("Talking Points: CIA Operations" 1999).

Bin Laden, as we now know, was actively plotting his next major attack—the hijacking of US aircraft. The plans for hijacking were going well and two of his men had successfully evaded security at a New York airport. The CIA believed that the plan was to hijack a plane to secure the release of the prisoners held for the 1993 World Trade Center attack ("Planning by Osama bin Laden" 1998). That was not his plan.

NOTES

1. That statement represents the bulk of what President Clinton has to say about Afghanistan in his memoirs. The subject is shockingly absent.
2. The El -Shifa Pharmaceutical Industries Company sued the US for damages, but on 8 June 2010 a US Court of Appeals ruled that it was a non-justiciable political question.
3. In an interview with *Al Jazeera* bin Laden (1998) suggests that he was warned by Pakistan. Asked about this possibility he replied, "As for the reports that we were pre-warned, I can say that thanks to God we have found a supportive people in Pakistan and one which has surpassed our expectations in the way it has supported us."
4. Rosenberg (2002, p. 459) provides an interesting critique of this article, erroneously cited as *"People Weekly."* Hirschkind and Mahmood (2002) critique the Feminist Majority Foundation's focus on the Taliban. Their critique is disingenuous and nonsensical. They argue that the Foundation should have acknowledged the role that the US played in Afghanistan's history. However, whatever role the US played in Afghan history does not change the way the Taliban treated women. They also argue that the Taliban's edicts did not affect too many people, which is true depending on the level of analysis, but the impact on the people it did affect was real and abhorrent. They ask the patently disingenuous question, "Why were conditions of war, militarization, and starvation considered to be less injurious to women than the lack of education, employment, and… Western dress styles?" (p. 345).
5. Ahmed Rashid claims that a direct satellite telephone link was opened to Mullah Omar and that, "The Afghanistan desk officers, helped by a Pashtun translator, held lengthy conversations in which both sides discussed various options [for bin Laden], but to no avail" (Rashid 2010, p. 140). He could be referring to the aforementioned single conversation or he does have knowledge of other talks through his own personal contacts (per his footnotes). Since there is no way to verify this claim until the 2020s when the relevant government documents will be declassified, I stand by the claim of this call being the only human contact.
6. In his Pulitzer Prize-winning book *The Looming Tower*, Lawrence Wright (2007, pp. 303–304) writes that Omar did actually agree to give Osama bin Laden to Saudi Arabia. Saudi Intelligence Chief Turki al-Faisel visited Omar to arrange this and later sent a down payment of 400 pick up

trucks. Omar reneged on the deal. This is likely what caused the Saudis' angry response.

7. The State Department attributed the perceived change in tone to the fact that the fax was dictated by Omar and not typed by Omar.

8. There is much more detail about this possibility that remains classified. However, in December 1998 the Taliban position changed again. Maulawi Wakil Ahmed told Eastham that "only Taliban courts are considered 'good' by the Taliban" (Eastham 1998c).

9. Sayed Rahman Haqqani should not be confused with Haqqani Network leader Jalaluddin Haqqani.

10. The resolution did not pass until 5 May 1999.

11. They held a second fundraiser in New York in October 1999.

REFERENCES

Afghan Women's Network. 1997. Afghanistan: The Biggest Prison for Women in the World. *Off Our Backs*, March 1997, 27(3), 12–13.

Albright, Madeline. 1998a. Message to the Taliban on bin Laden [Secretary of State Albright to US Embassy Islamabad]. 23 August 1998. US Department of State, document accessed at the National Security Archive, Washington, DC.

Albright, Madeline. 1998b. Afghanistan: Taliban's Mullah Omar 8/22 Contact with State Department [Secretary of State Albright to US Embassy Islamabad]. 23 August 1998. US Department of State, document accessed at the National Security Archive, Washington, DC.

Albright, Madeline. 1998c. Afghanistan: Message to Mullah Omar [Secretary of State Albright to US Embassy Islamabad]. 1 October 1998. US Department of State, document accessed at the National Security Archive, Washington, DC.

Albright, Madeline. 2005. *Madame Secretary: A Memoir*. New York: Miramax.

Anonymous. Redacted. 1998. Planning by Osama bin Laden to Hijack US Airplane; Successful Circumvention of Security Measures in US Airport [to White House Situation Room]. 3 December 1998. Central Intelligence Agency, document accessed at the National Security Archive, Washington, DC.

Ariana Afghan Airlines: Assets and Activities [redacted]. 1999. 29 July 1999. Central Intelligence Agency, document accessed at the National Security Archive, Washington, DC.

bin Laden, Osama. 1998. Text: Osama bin Laden's 1998 interview [with Al Jazeera]. *The Guardian*, 8 October 1998.

Boxer, Barbara. 1999. Senate Resolution 68. 106th Congress, 1st Session. 17 March 1999. Government Publications Office.

Burleigh, Peter. 1998. The Situation in Afghanistan and Its Implications for International Peace and Security. 84th Plenary Meeting of the UN General Assembly, *Official Records*, 9 December 1998.

Carlson, Margaret. 1999. All Wrapped Up with Nowhere to Go. *Time*, 12 April 1999, 153(14). Web.

Chang, Yahlin. 1999. Hollywood's Latest Cause. *Newsweek*, 6 December 1999, 134(23), 42. Web.

Clinton, Hillary. 1998. White House Remarks for Human Rights Day. 10 December 1998. *The Clinton White House*, National Archives. Web.

Clinton, Hillary. 2003. *Living History*. New York: Simon & Schuster.

Clinton, William Jefferson. 1998. Address to the Nation on Military Action Against Terrorist Sites in Afghanistan and Sudan. 20 August 1998. *Public Papers of the President*, Washington, DC: Government Publications Office, p. 1460.

Clinton, William J. 1999a. Remarks at the Sixth Millennium Evening at the White House. 15 March 1999. *Public Papers of the President of the United States: William J. Clinton, Book 1*. Washington, DC: US Government Printing Office, pp. 381–384.

Clinton, William J. 1999b. Remarks at a Democratic National Committee Reception. 19 March 1999. *Weekly Compilation of Presidential Documents*, 29 March 1999, 35(12), 485–487.

Clinton, William J. 1999c. Remarks at the Seventh Millennium Evening at the White House. 12 April 1999. *Weekly Compilation of Presidential Documents*, 19 April 1999, 35(15), 631–638.

Clinton, William J. 1999d. Remarks and a question-and-answer session with the American Society of Newspaper Editors in San Francisco, CA. 15 April 1999. *Public Papers of the President of the United States: William J. Clinton, Book 1*. Washington, DC: US Government Printing Office, pp. 551–561.

Clinton, William J. 1999e. Letter to Congressional Leaders Reporting on the National Emergency with Respect to the Taliban. 4 July 1999. *Weekly Compilation of Presidential Documents*, 12 July 1999, 35(27), 1283.

Clinton, William J. 1999f. Statement on the National Emergency with Respect to the Taliban. 6 July 1999. *Weekly Compilation of Presidential Documents*, 12 July 1999, 35(27), 1285.

Clinton, William J. 2004. *My Life*. New York: Alfred A Knopf.

Coll, Steve. 2004. *Ghost Wars: The Secret History of the CIA, Afghanistan, and bin Laden, from the Soviet Invasion to September 10, 2001*. New York: Penguin Press.

Crossette, Barbara. 1998. U.N. Delegate Will Visit Afghanistan to Push Talks. *New York Times*, 10 April 1998. Web.

Crossette, Barbara. 2001. Taliban Explains Buddha Demolition. *New York Times*, 19 March 2001, p. A9.

DCI UBL Update. 1999. 12 November 1999. Central Intelligence Agency, document accessed at the National Security Archive, Washington, DC.

Dhume, Sadanand. 1999. Mission Impossible? Taliban Tries to Mend Fences with the US. *Far Eastern Economic Review*, 11 March 1999, 162(10), 22–23.

Douglas, Carol Anne. 1998. Afghanistan: Feminist Pressure Prevents Recognition. *Off Our Backs* 28 (2): 5.

Dugger, Celia W. 2001. Muhammad Rabbani, Advocate of Some Moderation in Taliban. *New York Times*, 20 April 2001. Web.

Eastham, Alan. 1998a. Sitrep 6: Pakistan/Afghanistan Reaction to US Strikes [from US Embassy Islamabad to Secretary of State Albright]. 25 August 1998. US Department of State, document accessed at the National Security Archive, Washington, DC.

Eastham, Alan. 1998b. Osama bin Laden: Taliban Spokesman Seeks New Proposal for Resolving Taliban Problem [from Secretary of State Albright to US Consulate Peshawar]. 28 November 1998. US Department of State, document accessed at the National Security Archive, Washington, DC.

Eastham, Alan. 1998c. Osama bin Laden: Charge Reiterates US Concerns to Taliban Official, Who Sticks to Well-Known Taliban Positions [from US Embassy Islamabad to Secretary of State Albright]. 19 December 1998. US Department of State, document accessed at the National Security Archive, Washington, DC.

Eastham, Alan. 1998d. Osama bin Laden: Saudi Government Reportedly Turning the Screws on the Taliban on Visas; Haj May Be Affected [from US Embassy Islamabad to Secretary of State Albright]. 22 December 1998. US Department of State, document accessed at the National Security Archive, Washington, DC.

Eastham, Alan. 1998e. Osama bin Laden: Bin Laden Uses Recent Interviews to Assert Right to Use WMD, and to Threaten U.S. and U.K. over Iraq [from US Embassy Islamabad to Secretary of State Albright]. 28 December 1998. US Department of State, document accessed at the National Security Archive, Washington, DC.

Eastham, Alan. 1998f. Osama bin Laden: Chargé Underscores US Concerns on Interviews; Taliban Envoy Says bin Laden Hoodwinked Them and It Will Not Happen Again [from US Embassy Islamabad to Secretary of State Albright]. 30 December 1998. US Department of State, document accessed at the National Security Archive, Washington, DC.

Eastham, Alan. 1998g. Afghanistan: The Taliban's Decision-Making Process and Leadership Structure [from US Embassy Islamabad to Secretary of State Albright]. 31 December 1998. US Department of State, document accessed at the National Security Archive, Washington, DC.

Filkins, Dexter. 2001. The Legacy of the Taliban is a Sad and Broken Land. *New York Times*, 31 December 2001, pp. A1, B4.

Gannon, Kathy. 2005. *I Is for Infidel.* New York: Public Affairs.

Gutman, Roy. 2008. *How We Missed the Story: Osama bin Laden, the Taliban, and the Hijacking of Afghanistan.* Washington, DC: United States Institute of Peace.

Hirschkind, Charles, and Saba Mahmood. 2002. Feminism, the Taliban, and Politics of Counter-Insurgency. *Anthropological Quarterly* 75 (2): 339–354.

Hoban, Phoebe. 2000. Jay's Wife Fights for Afghan Women. *US Weekly,* 26 June 2000, 280, 38–39.

Inderfurth, Karl F. 1999. Pushing for Peace in Afghanistan [from SA—Karl Inderfurth to Secretary Albright]. 25 March 1999. US Department of State, document accessed at the National Security Archive, Washington, DC.

Inderfurth, Karl F. 2001. Face to Face With the Taliban. 23 September 2001. *Los Angeles Times,* p. M3.

Leno, Mavis. 1999. Dear Abby. *The Ottawa Citizen,* 23 July 1999, p. B6. Web.

Maley, William. 2000. The Foreign Policy of the Taliban. 15 February 2000. Report, Council on Foreign Relations. Web.

Maloney, Carolyn, and Dana Rohrbacher. 1999. House Resolution 187, 106th Congress, 1st Session. 25 May 1999. United States House of Representatives.

Mann, Judy. 1999. The Grinding Terror of the Taliban. 9 July 1999. *The Washington Post,* p. C11.

Mantilla, Karla. 1998. Afghanistan: Taliban Criticized: Leader Responds. *Off Our Backs,* March 1998, 28(3), 3.

Milam, William B. 1998a. Afghanistan: Demarché to Taliban on New bin Ladin Threat [from US Embassy Islamabad to Secretary of State Albright]. 13 September 1998. US Department of State, document accessed at the National Security Archive, Washington, DC.

Milam, William B. 1998b. Afghanistan: Tensions Reportedly Mount Within Taliban as Ties with Saudi Arabia Deteriorate Over bin Laden [from US Embassy Islamabad to Secretary of State Albright]. 28 September 1998. US Department of State, document accessed at the National Security Archive, Washington, DC.

Milam, William B. 1998c. Pakistan: Ambassador Raises bin Laden with Foreign Minister Shamshad Ahmed [from US Embassy Islamabad to Secretary of State Albright]. 6 October 1998. US Department of State, document accessed at the National Security Archive, Washington, DC.

Milam, William B. 1998d. Osama Bin Laden: GOP Official—Claiming Taliban Want to Get Rid of bin Laden—Reviews Three Options for Dealing with Him [from US Embassy Islamabad to Secretary of State Albright]. 7 October 1998. US Department of State, document accessed at the National Security Archive, Washington, DC.

Milam, William B. 1998e. Osama bin Laden: High-Level Taliban Official Gives the Standard Line on Bin Laden with a Couple of Nuances, in October 11

Meeting [from US Embassy Islamabad to Secretary of State Albright]. 12 October 1998. US Department of State, document accessed at the National Security Archive, Washington, DC.

Milam, William B. 1998f. Osama bin Laden: Coordinating our Efforts and Sharpening our Message on bin Laden [from US Embassy Islamabad to Secretary of State Albright]. 19 October 1998. US Department of State, document accessed at the National Security Archive, Washington, DC.

Milam, William B. 1998g. Osama bin Laden: Taliban Announce Cut-Off Date for Receipt of Evidence; GOP Official Says Taliban Growing More Intransigent [from US Embassy Islamabad to Secretary of State Albright]. 10 November 1998. US Department of State, document accessed at the National Security Archive, Washington, DC.

Milam, William B. 1999a. Afghanistan: Taliban Seem to Have Less Funds and Supplies This Year, But the Problem Does Not Appear to be that Acute [from US Embassy Islamabad to Secretary of State Albright]. 17 February 1999. US Department of State, document accessed at the National Security Archive, Washington, DC.

Milam, William B. 1999b. Osama bin Laden: US Points Delivered to Taliban and Pakistani Government [from US Embassy Islamabad to Secretary of State Albright]. 29 May 1999. US Department of State, document accessed at the National Security Archive, Washington, DC.

National Commission on Terrorist Attacks Upon the United States. 2004. *The 9/11 Commission Report: Final Report of the National Commission on Terrorist Attacks Upon the United States.* New York: W. W. Norton.

Rashid, Ahmed. 1999. Heart of Darkness. *Far Eastern Economic Review*, 5 August 1999, 162(31), 8–10.

Rashid, Ahmed. 2010. *Taliban: Militant Islam, Oil and Fundamentalism in Central Asia*, 2nd ed. New Haven: Yale University Press.

Richter, Gary W. 1999. Osama bin Laden: A Case Study. 6 December 1999. Sandia National Laboratories, document accessed at the National Security Archive, Washington, DC.

Rosenberg, Emily S. 2002. Rescuing Women and Children. *The Journal of American History* 89 (2): 456–465.

Rubin, Barnett. 1998. Testimony on the Situation in Afghanistan before the United States Senate Committee on Foreign Relations. *Council on Foreign Relations*, 8 October 1998. Web.

Simons, Thomas W. 1998a. Afghanistan: Reaction to US Strikes Follow Predictable Lines: Taliban Angry, Their Opponents Support US [from US Embassy Islamabad to Secretary of State Albright]. 21 August 1998. US Department of State, document accessed at the National Security Archive, Washington, DC.

Simons, Thomas W. 1998b. Sitrep 5: Pakistan/Afghanistan Reaction to US Strikes [from US Embassy Islamabad to Secretary of State Albright]. 24 August 1998. Department of State, document accessed at the National Security Archive, Washington, DC.

Soderberg, Nancy. 1998. The Situation in Afghanistan. 3952nd Meeting of the United Nations Security Council. 8 December 1998. *Official Records of the Security Council*, p. 7.

Talbott, Strobe. 1998a. Afghanistan: Taliban Convene Ulema, Iran and bin Laden on the Agenda [to Secretary of State Albright]. 25 September 1998. US Department of State, document accessed at the National Security Archive, Washington, DC.

Talbott, Strobe. 1998b. Osama bin Laden: Message Delivered to Taliban [Secretary of State Albright to US Embassy Riyadh]. 11 November 1998. US Department of State, document accessed at the National Security Archive, Washington, DC.

Talking Points: CIA Operations Against Osama bin Laden. 1999. 10 February 1999. Central Intelligence Agency, document accessed at the National Security Archive, Washington, DC.

United Nations Security Council Resolution 1214. 8 December 1996. Web.

Wright, Lawrence. 2007. *The Looming Tower: Al-Qaeda and the Road to 9/11.* New York: Vintage.

CHAPTER 5

The US and the Taliban Talk in Circles as the bin Laden Threat Grows

Abstract This chapter focuses on the increasing tension between the US and the Taliban, and the sources of frustration on both sides. The US and the Taliban continued to meet, but they succeeded only in talking passed each other—the United States explained why it was in the Taliban's interest to expel Osama bin Laden and the Taliban explained why they could not, despite many of their leaders' opposition to bin Laden's presence. It was increasingly clear that the US/Taliban relationship was going nowhere and that the only hope the Taliban had to be recognized by the US was to expel bin Laden—and that was never going to happen. To combat their poor public image, the Taliban mounted a public diplomacy campaign in the United States.

Keywords Afghanistan · Osama bin Laden · Sanctions · Taliban Unocal · United Nations Security Council · United States foreign policy

One year after the embassy bombings in Kenya and Tanzania, nothing had changed regarding the Taliban. They still insisted that there was no evidence Osama bin Laden was behind the attacks, and they still wanted good relations with the United States. Publicly, the US expressed great concern about women's rights in Afghanistan, but in private and in-country the concern was overwhelmingly focused on Osama bin Laden. The bin Laden threat was not just an American threat, and the United

© The Author(s) 2019
J. Cristol, *The United States and the Taliban before and after 9/11*,
https://doi.org/10.1007/978-3-319-97172-8_5

Nations Security Council was playing a growing role in its resolution. The world was now focused not only on the Taliban, but also on Al Qaeda. Though Al Qaeda was clearly irredeemable, the US held out hope for a good working relationship with the Taliban.

The US Alternate Representative to the United Nations, Nancy Soderberg, addressed the Security Council in the first open meeting on the conflict in Afghanistan. On diplomatic recognition, she said that, "If the leaders of the Taliban... want international recognition, they must respect the rights of their people." She called their treatment of women and girls "deplorable." She called on the international community to increase pressure on the Taliban until they "end their protection of terrorists" (Soderberg 1999, pp. 12–13).

The United Nations Security Council unanimously adopted Resolution 1267 on 15 October 1999. UNSCR 1267 demanded that Osama bin Laden be turned over to a country in which he would be brought to justice. The Taliban had until 14 November to comply with the resolution. In addition to the demand for bin Laden, it insisted that the Taliban comply with previous UNSCRs and end their sanctuary for terrorists and terrorist training camps. In her statement at the vote, Ambassador Soderberg said that she "hoped the Taliban would cooperate" and that, "The sanctions were limited and targeted very specifically to limit the resources of Taliban authorities and would, in no way, harm the people of Afghanistan" ("Security Council Demands that" 1999). The Taliban did not comply with the resolution and on 15 November, the UNSC imposed sanctions.

That day, President Bill Clinton froze Taliban accounts and restricted the landing rights of airlines "owned, leased, or operated by" the Taliban. He reiterated that the message to the Taliban was "unmistakable." They must close bin Laden's training camps and bin Laden must be brought to justice: "The people of Afghanistan have already paid a high cost in isolation because of the Taliban's continued harboring of this terrorist, and that toll will now increase" (Clinton 1999, pp. 2386–2387).

Revius Ortique was a prominent civil rights activist and the first African-American Louisiana Supreme Court Justice. President Clinton appointed him as an alternate delegate to the UN General Assembly. He was an ideal person to speak out against the Taliban. On the floor of the General Assembly, he said, "Persistent violations of human rights [by the Taliban], especially those of women and girls, remain a primary concern of the United States." The US expressed concern that opium poppy production had increased 43% in 1999, despite the Taliban's expressed support for the elimination of all opium poppy. He urged all member states to implement sanctions on the Taliban in accordance with UNSCR 1267. He said that the sanctions "have been carefully designed to minimize the impact on the people of Afghanistan" and that the sanctions are "targeted against the Taliban." The US had in fact given $70 million in aid to Afghanistan over the previous fiscal year (Ortique 1999, pp. 16–17).

One impact of the sanctions was to harm the image of the US in Afghanistan and Pakistan, itself the subject of US sanctions. US Ambassador to Pakistan William Milam gave a speech to the English Speaking Union in Lahore. In his speech, he recommended Ahmed Rashid's article "The Taliban: Exporting Extremism" (Milam 1999, par. 15).[1] Milam's goal was to push back at false claims that the UN sanctions were designed to hurt the Afghan people. One other false claim was that the US refused to meet with the Taliban, but Milam (1999, pars. 15, 31) pointed out that they had met with the Taliban "more than 20 times in the past year." The key fact was that all that the Taliban needed to do to get the sanctions lifted was to turn over Osama bin Laden.

Bin Laden was not the only terrorist interested in hijacking planes. On Christmas Eve, 1999, five hijackers commandeered an Indian Airlines flight from Katmandu to New Delhi. After landing in Pakistan and the United Arab Emirates, they flew on to Afghanistan and landed in Kandahar. India agreed to release three Kashmiri militants and the Taliban agreed to give the hijackers and the freed prisoners ten hours to leave the country. The Taliban were praised by India for their help, though the *New York Times* reported that some analysts suggested that, "given the Taliban's quest for international recognition," this praise might have been part of a deal between India and the Taliban (Dugger 2000, par. 25). The 1979 International Convention Against the Taking of Hostages requires that, if an act of hostage-taking occurs in a state, that state is obligated under Article Six to take the hostage-takers into custody for trial or extradition. The Taliban did not make any noticeable effort to track down the perpetrators of the hijacking, and the Americans wanted to meet and remind them of their international obligations.

Assistant Secretary of State for South Asia Karl Inderfurth, Special Assistants for Counterterrorism Nicole Bibbins and Michael Sheehan,

National Security Council Director for South Asia Donald Camp, and Ambassador Milam met for two hours on 20 January with Taliban Information Minister Amir Khan Mottaqi, Chargé D'affaires Sayed Rahman Haqqani, and translator Naim Dindar. Mottaqi flew from Afghanistan for the meeting. Sheehan pointed out the Taliban's obligations under international law to arrest and punish hijackers. The hijackers killed one of the hostages and escaped. Sheehan asked, "How can the Taliban make it clear to future terrorists that they will not be welcome in Afghanistan?" Mottaqi pointed out that they only gave the plane permission to land after clearing it both with the UN and with New Delhi. The Taliban condemned hijacking and terrorism in general. He said that India, the UN, and the Taliban gave the hijackers their word that they would go unharmed and "it would be un-Islamic" to break their word. Sheehan argued that a promise made under duress is not binding (Milam 2000a).

Sheehan acknowledged both that the Taliban did not want to harm the US and that, "they are not coordinating terrorist activities with Osama bin Laden," but said that bin Laden had been present in Afghanistan for so long that they are becoming associated with him and with his acts. Mottaqi spoke at length about the bin Laden problem, "We must find a solution to the bin Laden problem, no matter how, he said. It is a major problem for the Taliban. The mere existence of bin Laden in Afghanistan has caused Taliban relations with the whole world to deteriorate, including with countries like the US which helped us in the jihad." Then he tried a different argument for keeping him in Afghanistan. He argued that, "Having bin Laden in Afghanistan is actually to the benefit of the United States." If he were arrested, all of his sympathizers would "turn against the United States." He asked that the US not make such a big deal out of bin Laden, which only "makes more trouble for the US and for Afghanistan." He assured the Americans that bin Laden could not communicate with his followers. Mottaqi said that there were still three possible ways to deal with bin Laden: trial in an Afghan court; an ulema conference; or he would be overseen by the Organization of the Islamic Conference. It's shame that the US did not agree to those proposals, he lamented (Milam 2000a).

Sheehan replied that he understood that, "The Taliban believe bin Laden is... unable to do harm," and he acknowledged that the potential for a backlash against the United States was real. However, the US policy is not to let terrorists get away with their crimes. He acknowledged that, "there could be a short-term backlash if bin Laden were arrested, but in the long-term, the world would be a safer place if he were brought to justice." Sheehan endorsed all three of Mottaqi's ideas as interim proposals, but emphasized the necessity of compliance with UNSCR 1267. Even if bin Laden were as restricted as Mottaqi claimed, that would not negate the need to bring him to justice. Sheehan implored them, "I encourage you in all sincerity and friendship to find a way to resolve this soon. Despite your assurances that he cannot communicate with his network, we have evidence that he is planning acts of terrorism. We again encourage you to act soon" (Milam 2000a). The Taliban considered this to be a successful meeting and found that the atmosphere was "open and respectful" (Milam 2000b).

In New York, the Security Council had again taken up "the situation in Afghanistan." Ambassador Richard Holbrooke spoke to the Council at some length. He called Afghanistan "one of the great horror stories in the world today.... A vexing and tragic mosaic of suffering." He pointed out that the United Nations Development Program ranked Afghanistan last in the world on the issue of gender disparity. He said that recently there were "signs of modest improvement, at least in informal opportunities for girls.... [and] a trend towards improved access to medical treatment for women and girls, at least in Kabul." Holbrooke (2000, pp. 11–12) highlighted the international community's obligation to "implement sanctions on Taliban assets and flights."

By spring 2000, the Taliban position had further deteriorated. Inderfurth (2000) reported to Secretary of State Madeline Albright that, "The Taliban face growing domestic opposition, and their hold on power may be slipping." There were uprisings in Patkin and Herat. The Taliban fired civil servants because they could not afford their salaries. Smugglers were unhappy because UNSCR 1267 had shut down Ariana Airlines, their main conduit for illicit trade; and the Taliban were "frequently criticized for failing to stop an increase in burglaries and kidnappings." Albright hand-wrote on Inderfurth's memo: "This is encouraging" (Inderfurth 2000). In fact, UNSCR 1267 had led to the US seizure of over $250 million of the Taliban's money (Clarke 2000).

Even more encouraging was a meeting between Ambassador Milam and a still-classified Taliban who traveled from Kandahar. This meeting was "markedly different in tone," with "no tension or hostility." The Taliban representative did not question the evidence against bin Laden and was "primarily interested in receiving assurances that the bin Laden issue is the transcendent factor in US concerns about the Taliban, and that its resolution would represent a real inflection point in relations, rather than simply checking off one item on a lengthy laundry list." He expressed optimism that the bin Laden issue could be overcome, and was hopeful about the future of US/Taliban relations. He also said that there would be major decreases in the production of poppies now that Omar had forbidden their cultivation. This decree would be enforced because, "Mullah Omar does not issue many decrees." The representative also told Milam that a new edict would ensure that boys and girls are both educated, albeit not together (Milam 2000c).

Milam reiterated America's support for Afghanistan, and said that, "When the Taliban first emerged... the US was basically positive about the movement." It was not until some policies and human rights practices became problematic that the relationship had difficulties. The biggest problem was, of course, Osama bin Laden: "All in the United States Government are agreed that Osama bin Laden is our major problem with the Taliban—He is America's sworn enemy and will kill Americans again if he gets the chance." The source agreed with the ambassador's assertion that bin Laden posed a threat to the US. Milam pointed out that the US has good relationships with many countries with which there are major disagreements and outstanding issues. This was a key point. The US enjoyed good relations with many countries that had terrible human rights records, including the Taliban's former Saudi allies. The only thing preventing the Taliban from enjoying a good relationship with the US was bin Laden: "The one issue that cannot be subordinated or diminished is Osama bin Laden," but if they could get past that, "we would have a different kind of relationship" (Milam 2000c).

Milam's guest expressed his hope that the issue could be resolved. He also said that while the high-level Taliban knew that the US was not against them, many lower-level people did not know this. He suggested a goodwill gesture, even a positive statement about poppy reduction might work, or financial assistance through the Afghan Red Crescent. Milam (2000c) said he could make no promises, but would "see if anything could be offered." Milam remarked afterward that this meeting differed from previous meetings both in tone and in substance—The Taliban did not just repeat talking points. He recommended to Secretary Albright that the US make a small gesture like a statement in support of the drug ban, or a gift of two cars that had been left by past US government employees (Milam 2000c).

The new optimism about the Taliban was short-lived. In a New York City meeting with Under Secretary of State for Political Affairs Thomas Pickering, it became clear that the tone had again changed. The US had discovered that the nature of Omar's decree was to forbid consumption of opium, and that the Taliban were encouraging its growth. The "US... concluded that the Taliban responded only when pressured" (Albright 2000a). Thus the pressure needed to be ratcheted up.

While the Taliban were in the United States they also took time to meet with Unocal about the prospect of the proposed Turkmenistan–Afghanistan–Pakistan pipeline moving forward. The income from the project was important to the Taliban, but circumstances had changed and the pipeline was no longer a realistic prospect. UN sanctions made it impossible for the company to do business with the Taliban or in their territory. Additionally, Unocal had been advised "not to sign contracts until there is a recognized government in Kabul" (Crossette 1998, par. 8). Unocal Vice President for International Relations John Maresca said in his 12 February 1998 Congressional Testimony that, "Construction of our proposed pipeline cannot begin until a recognized government is in place." This is because an international pipeline requires government-to-government agreements, and those cannot take place if one of the governments does not recognize the other.

Ultimately, the domestic political pressure on Unocal from the Feminist Majority Foundation and its allies made working with the Taliban politically impossible. Rashid (2010, p. 174) writes, "Unocal first attempted to counter the feminists and then became distant in trying to answer their charges. It was a losing battle because these were American women and not foreigners." Feminist Majority co-founder Kathy Spillar said, "If Unocal is uncomfortable, it should be.... The more Americans learn about the Taliban's horrific treatment of women and girls, the more outraged they will become at the idea of an American oil company doing business there" (Prussel 1998, p. 2). The Clinton Administration had long backed the deal as a way to break Central Asia's dependence on Russia and to sideline Iraq and Iran. Years earlier, Unocal brought Taliban officials to the United States, where they held meetings on an oil rig in the Gulf of Mexico. The delegation visited Unocal's headquarters in Sugarland, Texas and received "VIP treatment and a shopping spree for luxury goods" (Vulliamy 1998, par. 2). Times had changed. Now, Unocal said that it had "no intention of rejoining a consortium to build a $2.7 billion gas pipeline from Turkmenistan to Pakistan" (Dhume

1999, p. 3). The company said that this was the result of falling oil prices, but others said pressure from women's groups played a part in the decision.

The oil issue is the subject of many conspiracy theories pertaining to the US role in Afghanistan. Perhaps the most common conspiracy theory is that the US supported the Taliban so that Unocal's pipeline could be developed, then when it looked like the Taliban would never consolidate power in such a way as to enable the construction of a pipeline, the US turned against the Taliban and sought its overthrow as early as 2000.[2] There is no documentary evidence to support that claim and the argument makes the mistake of conflating the government with a single company, which had long since lost interest.[3]

The feminist groups were not immune from the conspiracy virus. *Off Our Backs* hypothesized about the motivations for a meeting between the State Department and Rahmatullah including, "the desire to keep other Muslim sects from engaging in drug, gun, and terrorist activity in Afghanistan in order to clear the way for a proposed oil pipeline." The erroneous conclusion of the authors was that oil was paramount, and that "the Taliban is still being supported in some undetermined way by the US government" (Stato and Mantilla 2001, p. 1). It is deeply ironic that these authors had not recognized that they had largely won the battle to isolate the Taliban; though they had not succeeded in changing the circumstances on the ground for women in Afghanistan.

The Security Council took up Afghanistan again on 19 December 2000, and passed United Nations Security Council Resolution 1333. This resolution demanded that the Taliban allow UN personnel to access terrorist training camps to confirm their closure. It imposed an arms embargo on the Taliban and called on all states to close local Taliban offices and to reduce the presence of Taliban officials. The resolution passed 13-2 with China and Malaysia abstaining. Soderberg spoke out strongly against the Taliban and its continued sanctuary for Osama bin Laden. "The Taliban cannot continue to flout the will of the international community and support and shelter terrorists without repercussions," she said. "The Taliban policies have aggravated the already abysmal economic and social conditions of the people of Afghanistan," she continued, "It is important to remember that the cause of [their] misery is war, drought and the draconian policies of the leadership, not a ban on Taliban aircraft and assets" (Soderberg 2000, pp. 7–8).

It seemed as though the Taliban's chances of being recognized by the US and seated at the United Nations had fallen almost to zero. But there were those who argued in favor of recognition, and the Taliban decided to mount a new public relations campaign inside the United States. Former US Ambassador to Turkmenistan Michael Cotter (2000) made an argument in favor of recognition in a letter to the Washington Post: "Clearly, the Taliban's gender policies should weigh heavily in how we cooperate with or assist it, but those policies should not determine whether we recognize the entity that controls 95% of Afghanistan. Certainly, the Taliban would not be the only unsavory government that we recognize at least nominally."[4]

The Taliban knew that they had an unsavory reputation and launched a major public diplomacy campaign. Mullah Omar's advisor, Sayed Rahmatullah Hashemi, spoke at the Council on Foreign Relations, Atlantic Council, and Johns Hopkins' School for Advanced International Studies. He even appeared on National Public Radio's, "Talk of the Nation." The *Washington Post* called Rahmatullah, "cynical, irreverent, even witty at times," and said he spoke in "fluent, idiomatic American English" (Boustany 2001, p. A21). Outside the Atlantic Council 40 people, including members of the Feminist Majority, picketed Rahmatullah's speech (Stato and Mantilla 2001, p. 1). Abdul Hakim Mujahid, the Taliban envoy in New York, also made public appearances on behalf of the Taliban government. Mujahid spoke at Tufts University's Fletcher School for Law and Diplomacy, where he was questioned about the rights and treatment of women. He replied with a typical Taliban talking point that, "A woman's right to live a life free of violence and crime has grown stronger as the Taliban extended its control" (Beard 2000, p. A21).

Mujahid had been the Taliban representative in New York for two years. He lived in a Jewish neighborhood in Queens and his boys were enrolled in public school and his daughter at the Muslim Center Elementary School (Finnerty 1999, par. 11). Mujahid worked out of a "sparsely finished fourth-floor apartment" (Dhume 1999, p. 2). In an interview with the *New York Times*, Amy Finnerty asked him to respond to the Feminist Majority Foundation. Mujahid replied, "The Government in Afghanistan is running according to the will of 95% of the women there. If the campaign of the Feminist Majority were explained to Afghan women, Afghan women would find it ridiculous and insulting." Mujahid remarked that freedom of relationships in the US is "a good thing," but that the commodification of women in the US was unlike anything in Afghanistan (Finnerty 1999, par. 17).

The Clinton Administration held countless meetings with the Taliban. Most of these meetings followed the same script—the United States had great affection for the Afghan people and nothing in particular against the Taliban per se, so if the Taliban turned bin Laden over to the United States, there could be good relations between the two governments. Secretary Albright said, "Throughout, the problems we had with the extremist movement weren't due to any failure on our part to communicate clearly." The Taliban response was always to say that there was no evidence that bin Laden was behind the embassy bombings. They typically offered a compromise by which bin Laden would be tried either in Afghanistan or Saudi Arabia by a panel of both Afghan and Saudi judges. Otherwise, they continually insisted that Pashtunwali demanded that they protect bin Laden so long as he was their "guest." Secretary Albright (2005, p. 469) called these "lame excuses." They always assured their US counterparts that he would be kept from political activities and that they had him under control. The Clintonites were never convinced.

President George W. Bush was inaugurated on 20 January 2001. The Clinton Administration tried to warn the incoming national security officials about the importance of maintaining the focus on Al Qaeda. Richard Clarke (2000) wrote to incoming National Security Advisor Condoleeza Rice that, "Al Qaeda is not some narrow little terrorist issue that needs to be included in broader regional planning." The Al Qaeda training camps in Afghanistan formed, "the foundation of the worldwide mujahedeen network." 15–20,000 fighters had trained there since 1996 ("Afghanistan: An Incubator for" 2001). Despite the warning, former CIA director George Tenet (2007, p. 139) wrote that, "At the top tier, there was a loss of urgency."

And the situation had been urgent for some time. For years, the CIA had assets on the ground that were authorized "to try to capture bin Laden when the opportunity presents itself" ("Talking Points: CIA Operations" 1999), but their efforts were stymied by Washington. It had made a wide range of efforts to get bin Laden, including trying to work with potential Taliban dissidents. In one instance, Taliban intelligence chief Mullah Mohammed Khaksar, who had long opposed bin Laden's presence, arranged a meeting with the CIA's Peshawar station chief. He proposed that he overthrow Mullah Omar with American backing. The Americans in Peshawar consulted with Washington. No backing would be forthcoming, but they would covertly give him $5 million to over-throw Omar himself. Khaksar replied, "What was this $5 million? And who could believe they would get it, and what if you died before you could collect it? What then? For sure, your family would be killed. Who would look after your family, who would protect them? Right away someone would capture your family. They didn't understand" (Gannon 2005, pp. 61–65). The CIA was relentless in its hunt to find a way to get bin Laden at a political cost acceptable to the White House. And after many failed attempts, it was getting closer.

The CIA identified a camp near Jalalabad as "a development and testing facility for poisons and chemical weapons." The top priority for rolling back Al Qaeda was to weaken or eliminate, "The significant camp and facility infrastructure for training and safe haven sanctuary in Afghanistan." Sources inside Afghanistan reported that Al Qaeda was "buying the support of provincial leaders" for the Taliban. The CIA started running covert flights into Afghanistan in September 2000 and flew predator drones from Uzbekistan into Afghanistan. Its program would be massive support for the Northern Alliance to keep Al Qaeda tied down, the destruction of camps while in session, an expansion of the unmanned aerial vehicle program, and a recommendation to "explore possible efforts to remove the more extreme wing of the Taliban from power" as well as "propaganda and covert action to further divide the Taliban" (Clarke 2000).

On 8 February 2001, Mujahid and his deputy, Noorullah Zadran, an American citizen, visited newly promoted Acting Assistant Secretary of State for South Asian Affairs Alan Eastham, South Asia Pakistan/Afghanistan/Bangladesh (PAB) Director Jeffrey Lunsted and James Cole, the Afghanistan Desk Officer. Mujahid was there to deliver a letter from Taliban foreign minister Wakil Ahmed for the new Administration. The letter asked the Bush Administration to reconsider the Clinton-era policies towards the Taliban. The Taliban reverted back to their classic talking points with the hope that they would find a more receptive audience. They did not. The letter said that there was no evidence that bin Laden had been involved with terrorism. The Taliban complained that, "The previous administration used the issues of terrorism, drug traffick-ing, and human rights to isolate the Taliban." Mujahid informed the new crowd (same as the old crowd) that the Taliban wanted friendly rela-tions with the US and that bin Laden was an "inherited" problem. He again brought up the issue of diplomatic recognition: "If we expelled bin

Laden is there a guarantee that the Taliban will gain US recognition?" Mujahid also complained that they were not getting credit for reduction in poppy production, despite "billions" given to Colombia for the same efforts (Powell 2001).

Eastham was not having it. He told Mujahid that the US had "lost confidence with the Taliban on a number of issues such as, terrorism, human rights, and narcotics." He said that the Taliban needed to comply with UNSCR 1333 and come up with their own confidence-building measures. The US did not like sanctions, but they were necessary. He pointed out that the US had donated 100,000 tons of wheat to Afghanistan and that, "The US is not opposed to Afghanistan or Islam, but it is opposed to Taliban policies" (Powell 2001).

Mujahid spoke about the split within the Taliban. He said that, "80 to 90%" of Afghans disliked bin Laden "because of his Wahhabi background," and that, "Most of the Taliban leadership wants to be rid of [him]." Zadran chimed in to say that he wished the American missile strike on Khost two years earlier had killed bin Laden. Eastham replied that the goal was to bring him to justice without violence, but the US reserved the right to act in self-defense. Eastham informed his guests that as a result of the two UNSCRs the Taliban would have to close its New York office and cease to perform any diplomatic functions (Powell 2001).[5] The trappings of recognition were being eliminated.

Eastham and Rahmatullah appeared as the guests on the *Jim Lehrer News Hour* to discuss US policy on the Taliban. Ray Suarez asked Eastham to characterize the relationship with the Taliban. Eastham replied, "We don't have an official relationship with any government in Afghanistan. We do not recognize the Taliban.... At the level of doing business, however, we have contacts with all the factions in Afghanistan. That includes the Taliban. We talk to the Taliban when we get an opportunity and when we have things to say." Suarez asked if the Taliban are the de facto rulers, to which Eastham replied, "The reality is that the Taliban do control most of the territory of Afghanistan.... I think we are a long way from talking about full relations." Eastham discussed how the US can have a good relationship with the Afghan people but still have a more difficult relationship with the Taliban. He was blunt in his assessment of Taliban capabilities, "The Taliban government has shown that it can't govern. They have not addressed the needs of the Afghan people. They have not taken account of the wishes of the international community with respect to... terrorism, narcotics, protection of human rights.... After four and a half years, you really have to question whether they have the capability to govern or not. [The Taliban are creating] an impression that it is a place where every bad guy in the world can go and find relief and shelter." Rahmatullah said of bin Laden, "He has helped the Afghans with his own personal money.... So for the Afghans, he is a good guy. If we were to hand this good guy to the US, what kind of justification will we give to our people?" On the question of pipelines, Eastham said that, "It is not a major part of the calculus," but he recalled that when the Taliban came to power, they were accused of being tools of the US due to Unocal's interest in a pipeline (Eastham and Suarez 2001).[6]

The Taliban and Al Qaeda grew closer together, primarily because of Mullah Omar. Associated Press Reporter Kathy Gannon (2005, p. 32) writes, "The more isolated the Taliban became, the more bin Laden molded them into his likeness." Rashid (1999, p. 32) writes that, "Recent Taliban statements reflect a bin Laden—style outrage, defiance, and pan-Islamism that the Taliban had never used before his arrival." A 23 March 2001 CIA brief determined that the Taliban "needs bin Laden's money and fighters to wage its civil war." Interestingly, it reported that an exchange with the Taliban for bin Laden would be possible "after a Taliban victory and in exchange for diplomatic recognition and reconstruction aid" ("Afghanistan: Taliban Holding Firm" 2001). Another CIA analysis disagreed and said that the Taliban would support terrorist groups so long as Mullah Omar is in power: "Omar is formally committed to bin Laden's continued stay in Afghanistan." The report concluded that bin Laden would provide the Taliban infrastructure and development aid if the world did not ("Afghanistan: An Incubator for" 2001). In May 2001, the CIA concluded that bin Laden's recent increase in public profile might presage an attack ("Terrorism: bin Laden Public" 2001). When he was asked in an interview about any imminent attacks, he commented that he could not comment because the Taliban barred him from speaking to the press ("Terrorism: bin Laden Public" 2001).

The CIA was correct. There was an attack planned for May 2001, but the attackers needed more time to prepare (National Commission on Terrorist Attacks Against the United States 2004, p. 250). The attack was postponed until September.

NOTES

1. In this essay Rashid (1999) points out that the Taliban had a destabilizing effect on its neighbors due to the export of extremism and trained fighters, but "Washington's sole response so far has been its single-minded obsession with bringing to justice the Saudi-born terrorist Osama bin Laden— hardly a comprehensive policy for dealing with this increasingly volatile part of the world."
2. See Ahmed (2002) for a good overview of this perspective.
3. One piece of "evidence" to support these claims is the appointment of Zalmay Khalilzad as George W. Bush's ambassador to Afghanistan. Critics point out that he worked for Unocal, but ignore the fact that he was one of the few people with government experience who spoke the local languages and was well-connected inside Afghanistan.
4. For its part, Turkmenistan had decided early on to recognize the Taliban, but later reconsidered that decision due to uncertainty about the Taliban's staying power (Deutch 1996).
5. Mujahid was perhaps the only Taliban official to condemn the 9/11 attacks (Kumar 2013, par. 2).
6. The Rahmatullah quote in this paragraph comes from "Taliban Vows Revenge" (2001, pars. 18–19).

REFERENCES

Afghanistan: An Incubator for International Terrorism. 2001. 27 March 2001. DCI Counterterrorist Center, Central Intelligence Agency, document accessed at the National Security Archive, Washington, DC.

Afghanistan: Taliban Holding Firm on bin Laden for Now [Redacted]. 2001. 23 March 2001. Senior Executive Intelligence Brief, Central Intelligence Agency, document accessed at the National Security Archive, Washington, DC.

Ahmed, Nafeez Mosaddeq. 2002. America and the Taliban: From Co-operation to War. *Global Dialogue* 4 (2): 77–84.

Albright, Madeline. 2000. U/S Pickering Discusses Afghanistan, Democratization, and Kashmir with [Redacted] [from Secretary of State Albright to US Mission to the United Nations]. 20 November 2000. US Department of State, document accessed at the National Security Archive, Washington, DC.

Albright, Madeline. 2005. *Madame Secretary: A Memoir*. New York: Miramax.

Beard, David. 2000. Taliban Aide in US Defends the Record. *Boston Globe*, 27 October 2000, p. A17.

Boustany, Nora. 2001. In Fluent English, Taliban Enjoy Waxes Defiant. *The Washington Post*, 23 March 2001, p. A21.

Clarke, Richard A. 2000. Strategy for Eliminating the Threat from the Jihadist Networks of Al Qaeda: Status and Prospects. 29 December 2000. National Security Council, document accessed at the National Security Archive, Washington, DC.

Clinton, William J. 1999. Statement on United Nations Sanctions Against the Taliban. 15 November 1999. *Weekly Compilation of Presidential Documents*, 22 November 1999, 35(46), 2386–2387.

Cotter Michael. 2000. Letter to the Editor. *The Washington Post*, 23 December 2000, p. A22.

Crossette, Barbara. 1998. U.N. Delegate Will Visit Afghanistan To Push Talks. *New York Times*, 10 April 1998. Web.

Deutch, John M. 1996. Central Asian Reaction to Taliban's Takeover of Kabul. 9 October 1996. Central Intelligence Agency, document accessed at the National Security Archive, Washington, DC.

Dhume, Sadanand. 1999. Mission Impossible? Taliban Tries to Mend Fences with the US. *Far Eastern Economic Review*, 11 March 1999, 162(10), 22–23.

Dugger, Celia W. 2000. Hostages Land in India After Deal Is Made With Hijackers. *New York Times*, 1 January 2000. Web.

Dugger, Celia W. 2001. Muhammad Rabbani, Advocate of Some Moderation in Taliban. *New York Times*, 20 April 2001. Web.

Eastham, Alan, and Ray Suarez. 2001. Transcript: State Dept. Official Describes U.S. Policy on Taliban. US Office of International Information Programs. 29 March 2001. *Middle East News Online*, 30 March 2001.

Finnerty, Amy. 1999. The Taliban's Man in the U.S. *New York Times*, 21 March 1999. Web.

Gannon, Kathy. 2005. *I Is for Infidel*. New York: Public Affairs.

Holbrooke, Richard. 2000. The Situation in Afghanistan. 4124th Meeting of the United Nations Security Council. 7 April 2000. *Official Records of the Security Council*, pp. 11–12.

Inderfurth, Karl F. 2000. Taliban Under Pressure [from SA—Karl Inderfurth to Secretary Albright]. 1 May 2000. US Department of State, document accessed at the National Security Archive, Washington, DC.

Kumar, Sanjay. 2013. Abdul Hakim Mujahid. *The Diplomat*, 12 December 2013. Web.

Maresca, John J. 1998. Testimony to the US Congress House of Representatives, Committee on International Relations, Subcommittee on Asia and the Pacific. 12 February 1998. 105th Congress, Washington, DC.

Milam, William B. 1999. The U.S. Is Against Terrorism, Not Islam, Says Amb. Milam. 9 December 1999. *United States Information Service Washington File*. Web.

Milam, William B. 2000a. A/S Inderfurth and S/CT Sheehan Meet Taliban Representatives [from US Embassy Islamabad to Secretary of State Albright]. 1 February 2000. US Department of State, document accessed at the National Security Archive, Washington, DC.

Milam, William B. 2000b. Turkmenistan and Pakistan Predict War, Even While 'Working for Peace' in Afghanistan, and Continue to Support Taliban [from US Embassy Islamabad to Secretary of State Albright]. 13 March 2000. US Department of State, document accessed at the National Security Archive, Washington, DC.

Milam, William B. 2000c. Searching for the Taliban's Hidden Message [from US Embassy Islamabad to Secretary of State Albright]. 19 September 2000. US Department of State, document accessed at the National Security Archive, Washington, DC.

National Commission on Terrorist Attacks Upon the United States. 2004. *The 9/11 Commission Report: Final Report of the National Commission on Terrorist Attacks Upon the United States*. New York: W. W. Norton.

Ortique, Revius. 1999. Dialogue Among Civilizations. 78th Plenary Meeting of the United Nations General Assembly, *Official Records*, 10 December 1999, pp. 16–17.

Powell, Colin. 2001. Taliban Deliver Letter from Muttawakil; Say They Will Comply with Office Closing in New York [from Secretary of State Powell to US Embassy Islamabad]. 15 February 2001. US Department of State, document accessed at the National Security Archive, Washington, DC.

Prussel, Deborah. 1998. Feminists Take on UNOCAL. *The Progressive*, October 1998, 62(10), 2.

Rashid, Ahmed. 1999. The Taliban: Exporting Extremism. *Foreign Affairs* 78(6): 22–35.

Rashid, Ahmed. 2010. *Taliban: Militant Islam, Oil and Fundamentalism in Central Asia*, 2nd ed. New Haven: Yale University Press.

Security Council Demands That Taliban Turn Over Osama bin Laden to Appropriate Authorities. 1999. *United Nations Press Release*, 15 October 1999, SC/6739.

Soderberg, Nancy. 1999. The Situation in Afghanistan. 4039th Meeting of the United Nations Security Council. 27 August 1999. *Official Records of the Security Council*, pp. 12–13.

Soderberg, Nancy. 2000. The Situation in Afghanistan. 4251st Meeting of the United Nations Security Council. 19 December 2000. *Official Records of the Security Council*, pp. 7–8.

Stato, Joanne, and Karla Mantilla. 2001. Afghan Women Protest Taliban in Washington. *Off Our Backs*, April, 31(4), 1.

Taliban Vows Revenge if the U.S. Attacks. 2001. *PBS Newshour*, 14 September 2001. Web.

Talking Points: CIA Operations Against Osama bin Laden. 1999. 10 February 1999. Central Intelligence Agency, document accessed at the National Security Archive, Washington, DC.

Tenet, George. 2007. *At the Center of the Storm: My Years at the CIA*. New York: HarperCollins.

Terrorism: bin Laden Public Profile Might Presage Attack. 2001. 3 May 2001. Senior Executive Intelligence Brief, Central Intelligence Agency, document accessed at the National Security Archive, Washington, DC.

United Nations Security Council Resolution 1267. 15 October 1999. Web.

United Nations Security Council Resolution 1333. 19 December 1999. Web.

Vulliamy, Ed. 1998. US Women Fight Taliban Oil Deal. 12 January 1998. *The Guardian*, 011. Web.

CHAPTER 6

Conclusion: One Last Chance

Abstract This chapter shows that even after 9/11 the Taliban had the chance to expel Osama bin Laden, but they refused to do so. Many Taliban officials did want to expel bin Laden, but Mullah Omar was steadfast, and the US invaded Afghanistan. This chapter argues that the United States may have been able to prevent the Taliban/Al Qaeda connection if it had recognized the Taliban government in the time between the Taliban's conquest of Kabul and bin Laden's move to Kandahar. It argues that the case of the non-recognition of the Taliban government shows that the United States adheres to a constitutive theory of diplomatic recognition and recognizes new governments for political reasons.

Keywords Clinton Administration · Diplomatic recognition George W. Bush · Invasion of Afghanistan · Taliban · 9/11

The Portland Jetport is one of America's more pleasant airports, and on a sunny summer morning, it's about as nice an experience as modern American air travel can be. On the morning of 11 September 2001, Mohamed Atta and Abdulaziz Alomari took US Airways Flight 5930 to Boston's Logan International Airport, where they changed planes to American Airlines Flight 11—the first plane to crash into the World Trade Center. "11 September 2001" became "9/11." In total,

© The Author(s) 2019
J. Cristol, *The United States and the Taliban before and after 9/11*,
https://doi.org/10.1007/978-3-319-97172-8_6

19 terrorists boarded planes with the intent of hijacking them. Airplane hijackings had been a regular tactic of terrorist groups for decades. Al Qaeda introduced a new innovation: rather than use the hijackings to make demands and extract government concessions, they used them as the world's largest suicide bombs. The hijackers crashed two planes into the World Trade Center and one into the Pentagon. Realizing what was going on, the passengers on a fourth plane took control and crashed United Flight 93 into an empty field. Osama bin Laden had made good on his 1998 fatwa, "The ruling to kill the Americans and their allies—civilians and military—is an individual duty for every Muslim who can do it in any country in which it is possible to do it." The United States reaction was not swift, but it was severe.

President George W. Bush (2001a, p. 58) spoke to the nation that evening. He said that the US would, "make no distinction between the terrorists who committed these acts and those who harbor them." Deputy Secretary of State Richard Armitage met with Pakistani Intelligence Chief Mahmud Ahmed the next day and told him that, "President Bush had the Taliban very much in mind," during his remarks (Powell 2001a). Ahmed had actually been inside the US Capitol during the attack. He was there, ironically, to explain to Florida Congressman Porter Goss, the chairman of the House Intelligence Committee, what Pakistan was doing "to persuade the Taliban to hand over Osama bin Laden" (Rashid 2009, p. 21).

The 9/11 attacks marked a decisive turning point in US relations with the Taliban. On 13 September, incoming US Ambassador to Pakistan Wendy Chamberlain presented her credentials to Pakistani Prime Minister Pervez Musharraf. Chamberlain was blunt. She (2001a) told him that there was "no inclination in Washington to engage with the Taliban.... The time for dialogue was finished as of September 11." The next day, Armitage met again with Mahmud Ahmed and told him exactly what the US would need from Pakistan, including that Pakistan break diplomatic relations with the Taliban if they continued to harbor Osama bin Laden (Powell 2001b).[1] Pakistan would be a key player in what President Bush hoped would be a global coalition to support the elimination of Al Qaeda and the elimination of terrorist safe-havens.

President Bush spoke to leaders of Canada, France, Germany, Russia, and the United Kingdom. Powell spoke to myriad world leaders and foreign ministers. Powell even decided to "probe Iranian ability to work with us against the Taliban and Osama bin Laden." Plans were put in place to engage with dozens of countries around the world to build support. Powell wrote that the public diplomacy campaign would focus on "international coalition building" and "the human face of this tragedy." His long-term message was catchy and clever: "The world has changed: it is time to change the world" (Wong and Fujimura 2001). The "human face" was that of Afghanistan's women and girls.

Bush received from Congress an "Authorization for the Use of Military Force" (AUMF), which authorized him "to use all necessary and appropriate force" not only against those responsible for the 9/11 attacks, but also "to prevent any future acts of international terrorism against the United States" ("Authorization for the Use of Military Force" 1991). This vague and ill-defined authorization has since been used to justify US deployments at least 37 times in locations including Djibouti, Eritrea, Ethiopia, Georgia, Kenya, Philippines, Somalia, Syria, and Yemen (Weed 2016, p. 2). The AUMF has given three presidents broad powers, but it was originally written to authorize the invasion of Afghanistan and the pursuit of Osama bin Laden and Al Qaeda.

In a joint session of Congress, President Bush said that, "A collection of loosely affiliated terrorist organizations known as Al Qaeda" attacked the United States, and its leadership "has great influence in Afghanistan and supports the Taliban regime in controlling most of that country." Bush listed demands for the Taliban: "Deliver to United States authorities all the leaders of Al Qaeda who hide in your land.... Close immediately and permanently every terrorist training camp in Afghanistan and hand over every terrorist, and every person in their support structure, to appropriate authorities. Give the United States full access to terrorist training camps, so we can make sure they are no longer operating. These demands are not open to negotiation or discussion." President Bush (2001b, p. xv) could not have been more clear: "They will hand over the terrorists, or they will share in their fate." Bush had set forth the broad scope of what the Taliban needed to do, but there was still reason to talk to the Taliban. It was unclear if or how they would carry out Washington's demands, but if they were going to cooperate the two sides would need to coordinate.

The Taliban repeatedly, over many years, assured the United States that Osama bin Laden was not capable of committing acts of terrorism while he was under their supervision, but they were either lying or they were incapable of controlling him. The State Department determined that they would ask the Taliban to "turn over Osama bin Laden and all his associates responsible for terrorist attacks against the US, including senior deputies Ayman al-Zawahiri, Mohammed Atef, and Abu Zubaidah. Tell us everything they know about Osama bin Laden and his Al Qaeda associates, including their whereabouts, resources, plans for future terrorist acts, and access to WMD materials; Close immediately all terrorist training camps and expel all terrorists." They would have 24–48 hours to reply. The State Department considered three possibilities: (1) the Taliban would go after bin Laden themselves; (2) the Taliban would allow the US to go after bin Laden; or (3) they would refuse to comply. If they chose option three, then the US would "begin to work with our friends and allies to remove the Taliban leadership from power" ("Gameplan for Polmil Strategy" 2001). Planning for a possible military campaign would begin immediately, and Taliban-leader Mullah Mohammed Omar had something to say about it.

Omar gave a series of interviews explaining the Taliban perspective and making clear that there would be no negotiation with the United States. On the Taliban's Radio Shariat, he said Afghans should, "face any American attack with courage and self-respect" ("Taliban Vows Revenge" 2001, par. 9). He even spoke to Voice of America and explained why he could not turn over his friend Osama bin Laden to the Americans: "Islam's prestige is at stake.... If we [give up bin Laden], it means we are not Muslims.... That Islam is finished. If we were afraid of attack, we could have surrendered him the last time we were threatened and attacked [after the 20 August 1998 cruise missile strike]" ("VOA Interview with Taliban" 2001). There would be no reasoning with Mullah Omar.

The CIA also reached out to a Taliban contact, Mullah Abdul Qahir Osmani, who met with CIA Officer Bob Grenier at a hotel in Pakistan. According to former CIA director George Tenet (2007, p. 182), Grenier suggested that Osmani take them to Omar. Osmani rejected the suggestion. Osmani and Grenier met again on 2 October and Grenier suggested that Osmani "secure Kandahar with his corps, seize the radio station there, and put out a message that the Al Qaeda Arabs were no friends of the Afghans and had brought nothing but harm to the country" (Tenet 2007, p. 183). Again Osmani rejected the suggestion.

The goal of a potential war in Afghanistan was not clear. Should the war be fought until bin Laden was captured or killed and his training camps destroyed, or would the goal be to topple the Taliban? In Secretary of Defense Donald Rumsfeld's (2001b) "Strategic Guidance for the Campaign Against Terrorism," he discusses "plans and operations against state regimes that support terrorists, *possibly* including the Taliban or the Iraq Baathist Party" (emphasis added).[2] The US may not have decided if it would *topple* the Taliban, but it had no further interest in dealing with them.

However, it was perfectly willing to use Pakistan as an intermediary. Mahmud Ahmed went to Kandahar to meet with Mullah Omar. He asked Omar to allow Pakistani religious leaders, including former teachers of some Taliban officials, to travel to Afghanistan to talk about bin Laden (Chamberlain 2001b). Ahmed initially reported that the response was, "not negative" and that the "Islamic leaders of Afghanistan are now engaged in 'deep introspection' about their decisions" (Powell 2001c). Ultimately, however, this "last ditch effort to avoid military operations" was a failure. Omar would not accept any possible solutions to the now immediate bin Laden issue (Chamberlain 2001b); but Chamberlain had been wrong about the end of dialogue, the Taliban still had a chance to avoid war.

Secretary Powell sent an "eyes only" message to Ambassador Chamberlain. She was instructed to seek an immediate meeting with Musharraf or Ahmed to send a message to Mullah Omar. Remarkably, the Taliban's fate had not yet been sealed. The message was as follows: "We have information that Al Qaeda is planning additional terrorist attacks... If any person or group connected in any way to Afghanistan conducts a terrorist attack against our country, our forces, or those of our friends or allies, our response will be devastating.... It is in your interest to hand over all Al Qaeda leaders.... We will hold leaders of the Taliban personally responsible for any such actions. Every pillar of the Taliban regime will be destroyed" (Powell 2001d). The message could not be clearer, but Omar would not waver from his long history of ignoring American threats.

He may have ignored the threat because he thought that not only would the Americans, like the Soviets, be defeated in Afghanistan, but also America itself would be destroyed. In an interview with the BBC, Omar's position on the US was quite clear, "The current situation in Afghanistan is related to a bigger cause—that is the destruction of America.... If God's help is with us, this will happen within a short period of time.... [America] will fall to the ground" ("Interview with Mullah Omar" 2001). This statement might seem ludicrous, but it is important to remember that the Soviet defeat in Afghanistan was followed by the collapse of the Soviet Union. Omar's continued intransigence made it clear that a war was necessary to bring Osama bin Laden to justice and unseat the Taliban.

President Bush addressed the nation from the Treaty Room of the White House. He announced the beginning of the military campaign against the Taliban. The US would lead a coalition of more than 40 countries. Bush said, "On my orders, the United States military has begun strikes against Al Qaeda terrorist training camps, and military installations of the Taliban regime in Afghanistan." Bush listed the demands he gave to the Taliban at his joint session of Congress. "None of these demands were met. And now the Taliban will pay the price," said Bush (2001c, pp. 2–3). Secretary Rumsfeld (2001c) said the US would "terminate the rule of the Taliban and their leadership.... [and] would not commit to any post-Taliban military involvement" (Rumsfeld 2001c).[3] The war would be short and sweet.

The Bush Administration chose to use the Taliban's human rights record to help justify a war that few thought was unjust. One of Rumsfeld's talking points was that the Administration was "taking steps to assist Afghans who suffer from Taliban oppression" (Rumsfeld 2001a). On 16 November 2001, Laura Bush met with Feminist Majority Foundation head Eleanor Smeal, and the next day Ms. Bush argued on the radio that the war in Afghanistan was partially about the Taliban's treatment of women (Rosenberg 2002, p. 456). Historian Emily Rosenberg (2002, p. 457) writes that, "During the next several weeks, the US media embraced this theme of overthrowing the Taliban in order to rescue Afghan women and children." Ironically, both bin Laden and the Taliban had framed their own treatment of women as "rescue." The Taliban's oppression of women was not new. It was the centerpiece of their rise to power. The "liberation" of Afghanistan was certainly beneficial to women, but it was a fringe-benefit to a military campaign focused on Osama bin Laden and Al Qaeda.

The Taliban appeared to collapse quickly, though we now know that celebrations over their demise were premature. Anthony Cordesman of the Center for Strategic and International Studies argued that the Taliban's collapse came about due to the loss of support from Pakistan, as well as from the 60% of the country in which it was "virtually an occupying force." Moreover, the Taliban's force of 70,000 was too small to hold a country as large as Texas in the face of the American military. Cordesman (2001, p. 1) points out that, "Ideological or fanatic troops can often fight well in extended guerrilla combat but have a terrible record of holding up in conventional combat in the face of major firepower." Almost twenty years later it is clear that Cordesman was right.

The last Taliban fled Sangesar, on the outskirts of Kandahar, in the beginning of December 2001. The war was over and it appeared as though the Taliban had lost. Dexter Filkins (2001, par. 7) wrote that, "The Afghanistan the Taliban left behind is a sad and broken land." Filkins reported that some Taliban leaders claimed that they only needed more time to work out a solution to the bin Laden situation. One observer told him that, "The rank and file of the Taliban were opposed to bin Laden; even some in the leadership were" (Filkins 2001, par. 25). Laili Helms, a well-connected Afghan-American seen as sympathetic to the Taliban, said that, "Everyone I talked to in the Taliban wanted to hand him over... But Omar is an Afghan hillbilly who deals with the world at a tribal level and the United States never really went down to his level" (Stanleynov 2001, par. 30). That may not have been due to a lack of understanding, but rather due to the inaccessibility of Mullah Omar. Bin Laden presented a years-long problem for the Taliban, and they had had plenty of time and countless opportunities to expel him. Of his many discussions with the Taliban, former US Ambassador to Pakistan William Milam would later say, "Every time I met with these guys, I felt like I was going back to the fourteenth century. They never saw the connection between what Al Qaeda did and what their own fate and responsibilities were" (Filkins 2001, par. 29).

The Taliban government wanted to be recognized for many reasons, including pride; but the financial considerations were also important. It wanted access to Afghan money held in foreign banks, and it wanted to be able to enter into the government-to-government agreements necessary to gain the royalties from the potential Turkmenistan-Afghanistan-Pakistan pipeline. The Taliban officials never quite understood why their government went unrecognized by all but three countries.

American officials made every effort to explain US policy to the Taliban and to engage with them across multiple issues. *New Yorker* writer Ronan Farrow (2018, p. 173) writes in his book *War on Peace* that, "No one had sought a meaningful conversation [with the Taliban] for years.... American officials did take a number of meetings with the Taliban over the course of the 1990s but all were either perfunctory or focused on the narrow demand that the Taliban turn over bin Laden"; but American diplomats and intelligence agents made every effort to reach a *modus vivendi* with the Taliban. The potential for Afghanistan as a launching point for terrorist attacks was always a concern, but it was not until after the August 1998 Al Qaeda attacks in Kenya and Tanzania that the US became laser-focused on that "narrow demand"; but that focus was not unreasonable. The US knew future attacks were being planned, and preventing those attacks was a reasonable goal.

The United States may have been able to prevent the Taliban/ Al Qaeda connection if it had recognized the Taliban government in the narrow window between the Taliban's conquest of Kabul and bin Laden's move to Kandahar. US aid and assistance to the Taliban itself may have prevented the turn toward bin Laden, which was initially solidified by a $3 million cash payment. Recognition at that time would have been legally controversial, as the Taliban government had not necessarily established a level of the "effective control" necessary for recognition, but it was arguably legally justifiable. And while recognition may have been controversial using a declaratory theory of diplomatic recognition, it would have been less controversial under the constitutive approach to diplomatic recognition that the United States actually uses. The political nature of recognition, and the geostrategic benefit to recognizing the Taliban government, made recognition justifiable; but that benefit was not obvious to the Clinton White House, especially once the Taliban's treatment of women became well-known.

After Osama bin Laden moved to Kandahar and befriended Mullah Omar, all attempts to persuade the Taliban to expel bin Laden were futile. Ultimately, there was nothing the US could offer the Taliban that would change Omar's mind; and, partially because of bin Laden's support, nobody in the Taliban had the power to overrule or replace Omar. But that does not mean that the attempts were not worthwhile. Washington did not know it would not succeed, and even a small chance of success made the effort valid.

The Taliban case-study provides ample evidence that recognition is constitutive, at least to the United States. After the Taliban success at Mazar-i-Sharif, the case for non-recognition under either the Montevideo Convention or UN Agenda Item 61 was difficult to make. The Taliban government had "effective control" of 90% of the country and the bulk of the population. It may have been constantly at war with the Northern Alliance, but there are clearly recognized states, including India, Israel, Morocco, and Pakistan that have had ongoing violent conflicts for decades. Its territory was clearly defined and it had an independent foreign policy. Madeline Albright's September 2000 statement that even, "Taliban military conquest will not lead to the UN seat or international recognition," is further evidence of the political nature of the non-recognition of the Taliban government and of US recognition decisions more generally.

For the Clinton Administration, the Taliban's treatment of women made recognition impossible at the time when it could have made the greatest difference. In February 1998, Afghanistan expert Barnett Rubin (par. 12) testified before Congress that, "Opposition to the Taliban's gender policies accounts for much of the resistance to either recognizing them." It was after the 1998 embassy attacks, when the geostrategic benefit outweighed domestic political opposition, that the recognition of the Taliban government became more likely. The evidence shows that the Clinton Administration was willing to, at least temporarily, set aside the issue of women's rights and perhaps recognize the Taliban government, if only it would expel Osama bin Laden. But it takes two to tango. And after 1997 there was no real chance for a negotiated settlement. Mullah Omar said that if half his country "had to be destroyed to protect bin Laden, then so be it" (Filkins 2001, par. 31).[4] It would have been easy for Washington to write off the Taliban and resort to threats to get what it wanted, but it was not "all sticks, no carrots" (Farrow 2018, p. 173). In exchange for bin Laden, the US would have offered the Taliban government recognition, money, and assistance—even at the expense of human rights—and it gave the Taliban every opportunity to turn over bin Laden. After the 9/11 attacks, the diplomatic dialogue ended, but even then the Taliban had a final chance to turn over Osama bin Laden.

There *was* more that could have been done early on. The Clinton Administration could have recognized the Taliban after it took Kabul. That might have worked. It could have taken a more risk-friendly approach to political consequences and approved the various anti-Al Qaeda operations planned by the CIA. One of those might have worked. But short of a full-scale invasion of the country to get one man, after 1997 there was nothing that could be done to secure Osama bin Laden from the Taliban.

And a full-scale invasion of a country to get one man would be crazy.

* * *

Of course, it did not seem crazy at the time.

The invasion and occupation of Afghanistan was a failure. It failed to achieve all but the narrowest of objectives. It did not succeed in capturing or killing Osama bin Laden. It did not succeed in capturing or killing Mullah Omar. It did not succeed in destroying the Taliban. Many of the moderate members of the Taliban, who opposed the tacit alliance with Al Qaeda, either left the country or changed sides at the time of the initial invasion. The Taliban today is more unreasonable, intransigent, ideological, and extremist; and they controlled more territory in 2018 than they did at the end of 2002 (Constable 2018, par. 4). Over 111,000 people have been killed in Afghanistan since 2001 (Crawford 2016, p. 1). At the end of 2017, more than 15 years after the American invasion, there were more than 15,000 American troops in Afghanistan (Watson 2018, par. 2).

The circumstances for woman have improved in Kabul, but elsewhere, according to Human Rights Watch, "an estimated two-thirds of Afghan girls do not attend school." One 12-year-old girl told an investigator that, "The Taliban is near our house. If we go to school, they will kill us. If the government can provide security, we will be very interested to go to school" ("Afghanistan: Girls Struggle for" 2017). The situation in Afghanistan has gotten worse almost every year since 2010 and shows little signs of improvement. And the "human face" of the conflict has long since dropped from the headlines.

It was imperative for the United States to respond to 9/11, but the invasion and occupation of Afghanistan was unnecessary. The Taliban did not harbor Osama bin Laden because they themselves were terrorists. While Mullah Omar may have been taken in by bin Laden's pan-Islamic thinking, the Taliban's ambitions never extended much past Afghanistan. "[We will] make no distinction between the terrorists who committed these acts and those who harbor them" sounded good in the immediate aftermath of 9/11, but the Taliban and Al Qaeda were very different.

US recognition of the Taliban government would not have prevented 9/11; but it could have led to a different post-9/11 Afghanistan. Doing nothing was not an option, but the United States could have made clear to the Taliban leadership that it would be spared if it did not interfere in a ground operation focused on Osama bin Laden and the Al Qaeda leadership. Some Taliban may well have intervened on Osama bin Laden's behalf, and would have been eliminated, but others might have sat on the sidelines, or even taken the opportunity to overthrow Mullah Omar—knowing that they would have the tacit support of the United States. This type of operation may well have failed to capture or kill Osama bin Laden or Mullah Omar, but it could have avoided a seemingly endless, and endlessly destructive, war.

NOTES

1. It is possible to break diplomatic relations without withdrawing recognition of the government. It is difficult to withdraw recognition without an alternative government to which recognition can be assigned. Given that there had been no changes to the status quo in Afghanistan for years, and Pakistan had not wavered in its support for the Taliban, a withdrawal of diplomatic recognition would have been a difficult legal case to make.
2. This document is written in bullet points and is not entirely in full sentences. This quote is adapted from bullet points into sentences.
3. The US was prepared to overthrow the Taliban, but ill-prepared for what came next. Michael Waltz, a former policy advisor to Vice President Dick Cheney, wrote, "The US did not use the word counterinsurgency to describe the campaign in Afghanistan until 2006" (Waltz 2014, p. 350).
4. Some sources report that Mullah Omar married one of Osama bin Laden's daughters. If this is true it no doubt presented another insurmountable obstacle in Washington's effort to secure bin Laden.

REFERENCES

Afghanistan: Girls Struggle for an Education—Insecurity, Government Inaction, and Donor Disengagement Reversing Vital Gains. 2017. 17 October 2017. *Human Rights Watch*. Web.

Albright, Madeline. 2000. Pakistani Support for the Taliban [from Secretary of State Albright to US Embassy Islamabad]. 26 September 2000. US Department of State, document accessed at the National Security Archive, Washington, DC.

Authorization for the Use of Military Force. 2001. Pub. L. 107–40. 155 Stat. 224. 18 September 2001. Government Publications Office. Web.

bin Laden, Osama. 1998. Jihad Against Jews and Crusaders. World Islamic Front Statement. 23 February 1998. Web.

Bush, George W. 2001a. Address to the Nation on the September 11 Attacks. 11 September 2001. *Selected Speeches of George W. Bush*, The National Archives. Web.

Bush, George W. 2001b. Address to a Joint Session of Congress and the American People. 20 September 2001. *Harvard Journal of Law and Public Policy*, Spring 2002, 25 (2): xiii–xx.

Bush, George W. 2001c. We Are at War Against Terrorism. 15 October 2001. *Vital Speeches of the Day* 68 (1): 2–3.

Chamberlain, Wendy. 2001a. Pakistan: [Redacted] [from US Embassy Islamabad to Secretary of State Powell]. 13 September 2001. US Department of State, document accessed at the National Security Archive, Washington, DC.

Chamberlain, Wendy. 2001b. Mahmud on Failed Kandahar Trip [from US Embassy Islamabad to Secretary of State Powell]. 29 September 2001. US Department of State, document accessed at the National Security Archive, Washington, DC.

Constable, Pamela. 2018. Civilian Casualties in Afghanistan at Near-Record Level This Year, According to U.N. Report. *The Washington Post*, 13 April 2018. Web.

Cordesman, Anthony H. 2001. Why the Taliban Collapsed So Quickly. 14 November 2001. *Center for Strategic and International Studies*. Web.

Crawford, Neta. 2016. Update on the Human Costs of War for Afghanistan and Pakistan, 2001 to Mid-2016. Costs of War Project, Watson Institute for International & Public Affairs, Brown University.

Farrow, Ronan. 2018. *War on Peace: The End of Diplomacy and the Decline of American Influence*. New York: W. W. Norton.

Filkins, Dexter. 2001. The Legacy of the Taliban Is a Sad and Broken Land. *New York Times*, 31 December 2001, pp. A1, B4.

Gameplan for Polmil Strategy for Pakistan and Afghanistan. 2001. 14 September 2001. US Department of State, document accessed at the National Security Archive, Washington, DC.

Interview with Mullah Omar. 2001. *BBC News*, 15 November 2001. Web.

Powell, Colin. 2001a. Deputy Secretary Armitage's Meeting with Pakistan Intel Chief Mahmud: [Redacted] [Secretary Powell to US Embassy Canberra]. 13 September 2001. US Department of State, document accessed at the National Security Archive, Washington, DC.

Powell, Colin. 2001b. Deputy Secretary Armitage's Meeting with General Mahmud: Actions and Support Expected of Pakistan in Fight Against Terrorism [Secretary Powell to US Embassy Islamabad]. 14 September 2001. US Department of State, document accessed at the National Security Archive, Washington, DC.

Powell, Colin. 2001c. Deputy Secretary Armitage-Mahmud Phone Call—Sept. 18, 2001 [Secretary Powell to US Embassy Islamabad]. 18 September 2001. US Department of State, document accessed at the National Security Archive, Washington, DC.

Powell, Colin. 2001d. Message to Taliban [from Secretary Powell to Ambassador Chamberlain]. 5 October 2001. US Department of State, document accessed at the National Security Archive, Washington, DC.

Rashid, Ahmed. 2009. *Descent into Chaos: The U.S. and the Disaster in Pakistan, Afghanistan, and Central Asia*. New York: Penguin.

Rosenberg, Emily S. 2002. Rescuing Women and Children. *The Journal of American History* 89 (2): 456–465.

Rubin, Barnett. 1998. Testimony on the Situation in Afghanistan Before the United States Senate Committee on Foreign Relations. *Council on Foreign Relations*, 8 October 1998. Web.

Rumsfeld, Donald. 2001a. Thoughts on the 'Campaign' Against Terrorism. 2 October 2001. US Department of Defense, document accessed at the National Security Archive, Washington, DC.

Rumsfeld, Donald. 2001b. Strategic Guidance for the Campaign Against Terrorism. 3 October 2001. US Department of Defense, document accessed at the National Security Archive, Washington, DC.

Rumsfeld, Donald. 2001c. Strategy [from Donald Rumsfeld to Doug Feith]. 16 October 2001. US Department of Defense, document accessed at the National Security Archive, Washington, DC.

Stanleynov, Alessandra. 2001. She Spoke for Taliban and Now Pays a Price. *New York Times*, 27 November 2001. Web.

Taliban Vows Revenge If the U.S. Attacks. 2001. 14 September 2001. *PBS Newshour*, 14 September 2001. Web.

Tenet, George. 2007. *At the Center of the Storm: My Years at the CIA*. New York: HarperCollins.

VOA Interview with Taliban Leader. 2001. *The Washington Post*, 23 September 2001. Web.

Waltz, Michael G. 2014. *Warrior Diplomat: A Green Beret's Battles from Washington to Afghanistan*. Lincoln: Potomac Books.

Watson, Kathryn. 2018. Pentagon Takes Down Troop Numbers in Syria, Iraq, Afghanistan: Report. *CBS News*, 10 April 2018. Web.

Weed, Matthew. 2016. Presidential References to the 2001 Authorization for Use of Military Force in Publicly Available Executive Actions and Reports to Congress. 11 May 2016. *Congressional Research Service*.

Wong, Mark, and Paul Fujimura. 2001. Talking Points. 13 September 2001. US Department of State, document accessed at the National Security Archive, Washington, DC.

INDEX

© The Editor(s) (if applicable) and The Author(s) 2019
J. Cristol, *The United States and the Taliban before and after 9/11*,
https://doi.org/10.1007/978-3-319-97172-8
107

Printed in the USA
CPSIA information can be obtained
at www.ICGtesting.com
LVHW020234240124
769827LV00004B/36